APPRENTICED TO JESUS

APPRENTICED TO JESUS

DISCIPLESHIP PRACTICES FOR GROWING CHRISTIANS

Thomas R. Hawkins

DISCIPLESHIP RESOURCES

PO BOX 340003 • NASHVILLE, TN 37203-0003
www.discipleshipresources.org

ISBNs
Print 978-0-88177-628-7
Mobi 978-0-88177-667-6
Epub 978-0-88177-668-3

Apprenticed to Jesus: Discipleship Practices for Growing Christians
Copyright © 2013 by Thomas R. Hawkins

Scripture quotations are from the New Revised Standard Version Bible, copyright © 1989 National Council of the Churches of Christ in the United States of America. Used by permission. All rights reserved.

Library of Congress Control Number: 2013949363

Printed in the United States of America
DR 628

To Jan,
Colleague, friend, partner

CONTENTS

INTRODUCTION

As a teacher, consultant, and coach, I work with people and organizations that want to learn and grow. Some of the people and organizations with whom I work want to make incremental improvements in what they are already doing. For example, a group of teachers believes they are doing a good job in their elementary classrooms, but they have a few students whose reading skills are not improving. So they enroll in a two-day workshop to learn new techniques in reading instruction. These teachers hope to make incremental changes that will help them continue doing what they are already doing—only better.

This is called "single-loop" learning. In single-loop learning we ask the question, *How can I do just a little better something that I am already doing?* (See Hargrove [1995, 27–28] on the "three learning loops."). Throughout most of human history, incremental improvements usually worked. Change happened slowly and people never questioned if what they were doing was right. It was right if it worked, and improvements could be made so that it would work better.

Sometimes, however, people and organizations recognize that they must do things differently in order to thrive and grow. Imagine there are two congregations located in a rural area where the population has been declining steadily for generations. Church leaders know they cannot continue down the same path. Changes must take place if the congregations are to survive. Can each congregation pool its resources and share one full-time minister of word and sacrament? Can they merge with each other? When people or organizations learn something new in order to take a different approach, they are engaged in "double-loop" learning. Our two rural congregations' desire is to employ a different action strategy, not to incrementally improve what they are already doing.

Still other people and organizations recognize that they must approach change on a more fundamental level than implementing incremental steps or new action plans. Jack has been teaching high school speech and drama for a decade. He is frustrated by his school's emphasis on testing and quantitative data gathering. He also feels he has fallen into a rut as a teacher. Even the students seem to be changing in ways for which he is unprepared. Jack eventually quits teaching and takes a new position working with the Actors Guild. Jack did not make an incremental change in his life. He did not adopt a new action strategy for teaching his speech and drama classes. He became a different person in the fact that he totally changed his life's work.

Jack demonstrated "triple-loop" learning. Triple-loop learning asks the question, *Who do we want to be?* Jack did not attempt to improve upon what he was already doing. He instead transformed himself as a person. In triple-loop learning, people shift their points of view about themselves and their contexts. In turbulent environments, triple-loop or transformational learning is absolutely essential.

Unfortunately, we keep looking for single-loop learning in a world that requires triple-loop transformation. We know, at some level, that we are not getting the results we seek. We attend workshops on progress and improvement hoping an expert will give us a list of "ten best practices" (single-loop learning). Or we engage in strategic planning and develop a new action plan (double-loop learning). But what we really need is triple-loop learning. We need to learn to be a new kind of church for a rapidly changing, increasingly diverse, interconnected world.

This book invites you to join an adventure in triple-loop learning. It begins with the *why* questions and then addresses questions about *what* and *how*. This is not a book that will provide ten steps or five best practices. Neither will it describe how congregations and their leaders might develop new action strategies for improvement. We will find our way forward only through triple-loop learning that transforms our understanding of who we are as God's covenant people. As we enter Christianity's third millennium, we need to rediscover what it means to be the body of Christ in the world.

This book is based upon the belief that God calls the church to be a plausible sign, foretaste, and instrument of God's reign in human history. Responding to this call requires a shared-practice or apprenticeship approach to making disciples of Jesus Christ for the transformation of the world. Every aspect of congregational life empowers all participants to become both teachers and learners across their whole life spans in sharing faith. Together we are apprentices who are learning from Jesus Christ how to announce, teach, and live within an already present reign of God.

APPRENTICED TO JESUS

CHAPTER ONE

DISCIPLESHIP AND GOD'S MISSION TO THE WORLD

Called as Partners in God's Mission

Jesus' public ministry begins with two simultaneous actions. First, Jesus proclaims that the reign of God is at hand: "After John was arrested, Jesus came to Galilee, proclaiming the good news of God, and saying, 'The time is fulfilled, and the kingdom of God has come near; repent, and believe in the good news'" (Mark 1:14-15). Second, he immediately calls his first disciples: "As Jesus passed along the Sea of Galilee, he saw Simon and his brother Andrew casting a net into the sea—for they were fishermen. And Jesus said to them, 'Follow me and I will make you fish for people.' And immediately they left their nets and followed him" (Mark 1:16-18).

Matthew and Mark agree that here Jesus announces the inbreaking reign of God and simultaneously calls his first disciples. Luke introduces a slight variation when he inserts a day at Capernaum between these two actions, but the fundamental sequence remains the same, and it is surely not accidental. This sequence of events reveals an intimate tie between the call to discipleship and the nature and mission of the church.

It Takes a Community to Fish for People

The Gospel writers all agree that Jesus' first disciples fished on the Sea of Galilee before Jesus called them to "fish for people." The word *fishing* usually brings to mind a solitary angler, perhaps fly-fishing for trout in a mountain stream. Or we imagine someone sitting alone in a boat on a quiet, mist-covered lake. But fishing on the Sea of Galilee would not have been a solitary enterprise. It involved net fishing, which required a team of people working together. With carefully coordinated effort, the crew cast a large net from the boat and held it open so as many fish as possible could swim into the net. It took the whole crew, holding the corners and sides of the net, to pull it into the boat so no fish could escape.

When Jesus called his first disciples to fish for people, he was summoning them to a task that no one working alone could accomplish. It took a team to fish for people. There was never a time when Jesus had only one disciple. From the very beginning of his ministry, Jesus was surrounded by a community of disciples. Christian faith is both deeply personal and radically communal.

Why is Jesus' announcement of God's reign inseparable from Jesus calling of his disciples? We are so accustomed to thinking of God's reign as a future reality that we have difficulty recognizing and interpreting the many passages where Jesus describes it as an already present reality. Yet Jesus repeatedly makes precisely this claim, explaining the link between the call to discipleship and the announcement of God's reign.

God's reign, according to Jesus, is an already present reality among us. It is not a kingdom that will arrive someday in the distant future. Jesus' announcement captured in Mark's Gospel is in the perfect indicative tense in the Greek, not the future tense or even the present tense: God's reign "has come" near, not "will come near." If this kingdom is already present in human history, then it must be visible in a concrete, historical way that people can validate in their own experiences. Otherwise, Jesus was either delusional or toying with people's hopes when he said God's reign has come and is already among us.

Jesus simultaneously announces God's reign and gathers a community of disciples so that a concrete, visible social reality exists where people can experience this inbreaking kingdom. The community called and gathered by Jesus, the church, is not to be equated with God's reign; but it is a sign, foretaste, and instrument of God's reign. Jesus invites all humanity into a new social order, a covenant community of his disciples. This community participates in the kingdom's blessings. It celebrates the hopes of the kingdom's full establishment on earth. Jesus' disciples, who have already entered this kingdom, now announce, receive, and welcome others into it.

When John the Baptist's disciples ask Jesus, "Are you the one who is to come, or are we to wait for another?" Jesus says to them, "Go and tell John what you hear and see: the blind receive their sight, the lame walk, the lepers are cleansed, the deaf hear, the dead are raised, and the poor have good news brought to them" (Matt. 11:2-5). Since Jesus sent out his disciples two by two to heal, preach, and teach in his name (Matt. 10), Jesus is clearly not speaking only of his own personal ministry. He is instead referring to the disciples' shared ministry with him. If you want to know whether God's kingdom has arrived, Jesus tells John the Baptist's disciples, just look at what my followers are doing in my name.

Because God's reign is already present among us in the form of a concrete, historical community, it is necessarily a collaborative kingdom. It is not something that will happen in the distant future and for which we can only wait passively. God's reign is already among us. God is waiting to welcome us into this already present kingdom, but we have to receive it, enter into it, live from it: "Ask, and it will be given you; search, and you will find; knock, and the door will be opened for you. For everyone who asks receives, and everyone who searches finds, and for everyone who knocks, the door will be opened. . . . How much more will your Father in heaven give good things to those who ask him!" (Matt. 7:7-8, 11). God's reign is already present among humankind, but it can be established only when people choose to enter and dwell within it.

For Jesus, God's kingdom is not a physical place outside time and space. We cannot equate God's reign with "heaven" or someplace we go when we die. The reign of God is more like a household, a community, a social "happening" where healing, reconciliation, nourishment, and hope are unexpectedly available and gladly received. To be a disciple of Jesus Christ is to dwell within, invite, and welcome others into such a social space, no matter how transitory or ephemeral it seems. God may offer the kingdom to humankind, but we must enter it, dwell within it, and thus establish it on earth as it already is in heaven: "For where two or three are gathered in my name, I am there among them" (Matt. 18:20). God's reign cannot be localized in one place or one group or one institution: "The kingdom of God is not coming with things that can be observed; nor will they say, 'Look, here it is!' or 'There it is!' For, in fact, the kingdom of God is among you" (Lk. 17:20-21). We do not possess God's kingdom; it possesses us.

Jesus calls his followers to live together in ways that are a sign, foretaste, and instrument of God's already present, collaborative kingdom. Jesus' followers are called out of the world to be the church. Disciples of Jesus Christ are those who have already received, entered, and now dwell within God's reign and so establish it upon the earth: "In him the whole structure is joined together and grows into a holy temple in the Lord; in whom you also are built together spiritually into a dwelling place for God" (Eph. 2:21-22). God's reign has already begun, and it can be experienced, however partially and imperfectly, in the community of Jesus' disciples here on earth, the body of Christ.

Discipleship and God's Mission to Heal a Spoiled Creation

A collaborative community cannot exist through coercion or compulsion. God does not force or compel us to enter the kingdom. We choose to enter it and thus establish it among us. Collaboration signifies presence, presence requires relationship, and relationship involves bonds of trust and care. These qualities suggest a third characteristic of God's reign and therefore of Christian discipleship—self-giving, non-coercive love. Paul says in Ephesians, "I pray that, according to the riches of his glory, he may grant that you may be strengthened in your inner being with power through his Spirit, and that Christ may dwell in your hearts through faith, as you are being rooted and grounded in love. I pray that you may have the power to comprehend, with all the saints, what is the breadth and length and height and depth, and to know the love of Christ that surpasses knowledge, so that you may be filled with all the fullness of God" (3:16-19). The purpose of discipleship is to grow in a love that transforms the world.

Never One Disciple but Always One Mission

Jesus never has just one disciple, but he always has just one mission: God's eternal mission to heal a creation meant for love but disfigured by hostility and division. God's mission is to reestablish a world where "the wolf shall live with the lamb, the leopard shall lie down with the kid, the calf and the lion and the fatling together, and a little child shall lead them" (Isa. 11:6).

In all three synoptic Gospels, Jesus and his disciples crisscross the Sea of Galilee in their boats. Jewish villages dominate the west side of the Sea of Galilee; but the east side is Gentile. Crossing the Sea of Galilee, shuttling back and forth between Jew and Gentile, Jesus calls his disciples to participate in forming a new people of God no longer characterized by separation and division. Mark, for example, shows Jesus miraculously feeding a crowd of people on the Jewish side of the Sea of Galilee (Mark 6:30-44). He then crosses to the other side of the sea where he feeds a crowd of Gentiles (7:31; 8:1-9). He then performs a healing on the Gentile side, and later he performs two more healings on the Jewish side (5:1-43). Jesus' sea crossings are signs of God's mission to reconcile a world separated by hostility and suspicion.

By calling together a community of disciples skilled in navigating between separated peoples, Jesus' ministry bridges the gulf between people previously divided by enmity and suspicion. This mission fulfills the Hebrew prophets' description of God's mission to the world: "In days to come the mountain of the LORD's house shall be established as the highest of the mountains, and shall be raised above the hills; and the nations shall stream to it. Many peoples shall come and say, 'Come, let us go up to the mountain of the LORD . . . that [God] may teach us [God's] ways and that we may walk in [God's] paths'" (Isa. 2:2-3).

The announcement that God's kingdom has come near is also the announcement that God intends to overcome the violence and hostility unleashed when Cain killed Abel, a divisive violence that extended beyond the human race to the desecration and destruction of creation itself. Jesus' mission restores the possibility of a nonviolent, noncoercive world characterized by harmony and shalom. As Paul wrote to the Ephesians, "You are no longer strangers and aliens, but you are citizens with the saints and also members of the household of God, built upon the foundation of the apostles and prophets, with Christ Jesus himself as the cornerstone." (Eph. 2:19-20).

Paradise to Pain: The Disfigurement of God's Original Creation

This kingdom quality of shalom, or peace with justice, stands in stark contrast to how we usually experience our world. We typically encounter it as a violent and hostile place because it no longer reflects God's original intentions. The first chapters of Genesis describe the world as God created it. God placed the first man and first woman in a garden, where they lived harmoniously with the earth and its rhythms. They cultivated a garden of beauty and fruitfulness. They lived in a caring relationship with each other and could say of each other, "This at last is bone of my bones and flesh of my flesh" (Gen. 2:23). As human beings, we are meant to live in peace with all living creatures, for we have named them and know them as well as we know ourselves. We are made for intimacy with God, who walks with us and speaks directly to us (Gen. 3:8).

The author of Genesis then describes how this world became disfigured and marred. In Genesis 3, the serpent awakens the woman's desire to be like God, possessing what God already enjoys. The serpent tells the woman, "When you eat of [the fruit of the tree] your eyes will be opened, and you will be like God, knowing good and evil" (v. 5). Once it has aroused the desire to imitate God, the serpent next converts God from a friend into a rival. The serpent sows the seeds of rivalry and suspicion by suggesting that God sees the woman and man not as companions but as competitors. Perhaps, the serpent insinuates, God is misleading Adam and Eve with a lie, telling them that they will die if they eat from the tree, because God already fears them as potential rivals for power and wisdom. To the contrary, "you will not die," says the serpent (Gen. 3:4).

The first man and woman fell into the serpent's trap. Wanting to be like God stirred up in them the desire to possess what God possesses. This desire converted companionship into competition, which engendered rivalry, suspicion, and hostility. The woman misled the man. The man betrayed the woman. Work meant for beauty and fruitfulness became meaningless toil. Animals once known so intimately became a danger and a threat. So God withdrew.

Unleashed into the world, desire, imitation, and rivalry spread like a contagious virus. They contaminated all they touched, especially human relationships. This pattern of desire, imitation, rivalry, and hostility repeats itself in all our relationships. We become face readers and mind readers. We look at someone else—someone we admire, depend upon, or perhaps even love—and we want to be just like them. So we imitate their desires. We want to possess what they have because we long to be just like them. But, once we mimic their desires, our relationship to them changes radically. They become rivals. Our admiration for them turns to envy, and envy engenders fear and distrust. Rather than desiring to imitate them because we love them, we now fear them. A destructive ricocheting of rivalry and suspicion degenerates into hostility and violence. The consequences of this process reverberate throughout all creation. The serpent's seduction reaches its ultimate conclusion when Cain kills Abel, unleashing murderous violence into the world.

According to scripture, all God's subsequent efforts in history have been aimed at repairing a broken creation. This is God's mission to the world. Just as the Bible begins with God's good creation tragically disfigured, it ends with a picture of creation renewed. God's mission is fulfilled. God's kingdom comes. The New Jerusalem in the book of Revelation is not just a world city; it is the city as the world. John describes it as 12,000 stadia, or 1,500 miles, long and 12,000 stadia, or 1,500 miles, wide: as big as the whole Mediterranean world (Rev. 21:15-16). And it extends another 1,500 miles into space. It includes not only the human world but also the whole cosmos. All nations will live together in peace in this New Jerusalem. Even nature itself is renewed and healed. Streams of water flow from the throne of God to water the trees, whose leaves are for the healing of the nations (Rev. 22:2). There is no temple in the city, because God once again dwells in such intimacy with humankind that no temple is needed (Rev. 21:22). The New Jerusalem is Paradise restored and renewed.

Called to Announce and Embody a New Creation

This is God's mission to the world: to heal its endless cycles of desire, rivalry, and violence. It is a vision of shalom, a world of peace with justice. God sent Jesus Christ into the world on behalf of this mission. Christ calls disciples into a covenant community to whom he entrusts this same mission. The call to discipleship is always for the sake of God's transforming mission. It is not for special privilege or for our own individual spiritual comfort. God did not send Jesus into the world simply to save individual souls. God sent Jesus to call disciples who would participate in God's own mission to transfigure a creation marred by sin and violence. Jesus revealed God's passion for the world as well as God's ultimate purpose for the world: all creatures living once more in a relationship of trust and harmony with God and one another. For the reign of God is joy and peace in one another. This mission, however, did not begin with Jesus' calling his disciples. It started much earlier.

GOD'S IMPROBABLE PLAN

God begins in a small way. There must be a single place and people where God's mission begins. Starting in one small place, God intends this new beginning to spread slowly through all creation. It will not spread by compulsion or coercion, which themselves are rooted in the serpent's seduction. It grows only through freedom, collaboration, and compassion.

God begins this way because God has plenty of time. Humans have only a limited view of time. We want to see the fruit of our labors in our own lifetimes. Our desire to see quick results means we try to change the world through coercion or compulsion. But for God, a thousand years are nothing more than the passing of one night (Ps. 90:4). God can thus work patiently in human history. God's plan can work across many generations and lifetimes. God takes a long view because God respects human freedom. God will not use the serpent's tools to undo the serpent's destruction of a good creation.

Since creation was marred by human action, God's new creation must begin with humans and their relationships in community. God will not compel people into this new creation. They can only be drawn by the lure of what they experience among a people of harmony and wholeness who live amid a sea of rivalry, hostility, and violence.

God Calls Abraham and Sarah

In Genesis 12, we move from a story of disobedience to one of obedience. Through Sarah and Abraham, God makes a new beginning. God blesses the earth through a collaborative covenant with Abraham and Sarah's household. They become partners with God in God's mission to redeem the world: "I will bless you, and make your name great, so that you will be a blessing. . . . In you all the families of the earth shall be blessed" (Gen. 12:3).

God's covenant with Abraham and Sarah's household reverses the serpent's pattern of desire, rivalry, and violence. Abraham refuses to compete for land and herds with his nephew Lot. He does not see Lot as a rival but treats him as a fellow creature with whom he lives in mutuality and trust: "Abram said to Lot, 'Let there be no strife between you and me, and between your herders and my herders; for we are kindred'" (Gen. 13:8). Relationships in God's new household are like the relationship between Abraham and Lot, noncoercive and characterized by freedom and care, not suspicion and rivalry. The descendants of Abraham and Sarah eventually find themselves in Egypt, a land of pyramids and priests where it is easy to forget God's vision of a renewed creation.

Moses Calls an Improbable People to Come and Follow

Egypt is not just a place on ancient maps. Egypt is every place where coercive power and hierarchy dominate. It is every human society in which the cycle of rivalry and suspicion repeats its bloody history. A pharaoh arose who "did not know Joseph" (Ex. 1:8) and sees the Israelites as rivals for power. Pharaoh's fears trigger an intensifying cycle of suspicion and hostility that ultimately reduces Abraham and Sarah's descendants to slavery. Pharaoh's fear and hostility engender brutality and violence as he orders all male children to be killed (Ex. 1:16).

Into this perfect organization of coercive power and violence, God calls Moses to lead the people out of Egypt. Moses' first instinct is to challenge violence with more violence. He tries to stop the beating of a Hebrew slave by killing the Egyptian overseer. He wants to create a new world by using the old creation's tools and methods. But God instead calls Moses to form a new community built around radically different principles. The Sinai covenant embraced a view of the world fundamentally different from Egypt's pyramids of power. The Ten Commandments required Israel to renounce envy and the desire to covet or steal what others possessed, thus rejecting the serpent's original seduction of humankind through mimetic desire and envy. The Ten Commandments specifically prohibited the ultimate expression of violence: taking another person's life. They also enjoined upon Israel relationships of care and compassion toward one's parents, toward strangers, and even toward livestock that deserved a day of rest and refreshment. The sabbath itself is a sign of a healed creation, harkening back to Genesis 1, where God rests on the seventh day and proclaims creation "very good" (Gen. 1:31).

The Sinai covenant sought to create a community freed from the corrosive dynamics of suspicion and hostility: "You shall not spread a false report. . . . When you bear witness in a lawsuit, you shall not side with the majority so as to pervert justice" (Ex. 23:1-2). One's neighbors are not rivals and competitors but fellow creatures deserving our forgiveness and help: "When you come upon your enemy's ox or donkey going astray, you shall bring it back. When you see the donkey of one who hates you lying under its burden and you would hold back from setting it free, you must help to set it free" (Ex. 23:4-5).

The Sinai covenant enshrined God's mission not in abstract ideals but in a concrete historical community of people among whom God's original intent for creation could be realized. The Torah was not given just to create righteous individuals. It was given to engender a righteous and just society. Israel was to be a concrete, historical community that made God's reign plausible to all who encountered it. Israel had no king because God reigned over God's people; and God's rule, unlike Pharaoh's, was collaborative and noncoercive.

The call to be a disciple is always a call to an exodus from whatever Egypt in which we find ourselves. Egypt is every society dominated by pyramids of power, cities of the dead, coercive labor, violent overseers, and armed border guards. Egypt is suffocating and oppressive because it organizes efficiently and comprehensively the old creation's envy and desire, subjugating these drives to the goals of consumption and production.

Disciples are called to form a new community organized around God's reign over all creation. This new community is the leverage point from which God intends to transform an old creation marred by disobedience. Disciples are not called simply to enjoy a new quality of personal life. They are also called so all humanity can encounter, receive, and enter God's reign amid a creation made new.

The community gathered around Sinai's covenant is a visible social reality in which people live in a different way and treat one another differently than they are treated elsewhere in the world. It is a concrete social space where God rules in a way that is very distinct from how human kings ordinarily exercise their rule. Matthew's Gospel would later portray Jesus as a new Moses. Just as Moses called people into a community that exhibited a new pattern of living, Jesus would call his disciples into a renewed community that manifested God's kingdom amid the kingdoms of this world.

David and Solomon: A Risky Experiment

With the kingship of David, Solomon, and their descendants, Israel abandons God's call to be a visible community where God's new creation has already begun. Israel instead embarks on a risky experiment in which God's covenant people are no longer identified as an alternative, contrasting community to a world characterized by imitative desire, hostile rivalry, and violent coercion. Israel decides to become like the fallen world around it. The people come to the prophet Samuel and say, "Appoint for us, then, a king to govern us, like other nations" (1 Sam. 8:5). Israel's request for a king amounts to a rejection of God's style of rule, a style of rule where people live in proper relationship to one another and all creation.

A king like the kings in the nations around them, Samuel prophesies, would take Israel's sons and appoint them to his chariots. A king would take their fields and vineyards and orchards from them and give them to his courtiers. He would take their herds and flocks and make them his slaves (1 Sam. 8:10-18). In other words, the kingship Israel wanted would reintroduce all the trappings of coercion, coveting, exploitation, and violence that God's covenants with Abraham and Moses sought to overturn. The books of 1 and 2 Kings chronicle Israel's slow transformation into just another minor kingdom among the great powers of its day.

The prophets repeatedly protest against Israel's abandonment of the Sinai covenant. They see Israel's kingship as a dead-end experiment. David, Solomon, and their descendants become another version of Egypt's violence and oppression. According to the prophets, God's reign over a renewed creation resembles neither an Egypt nor a Jerusalem. With the collapse of the Davidic kingship, God's experiment in restoring God's creation seemed to have reached a dead end. One lesson of this failed experiment was that the call to participate in God's reign is never easy, never certain, and always under threat.

A NEW BEGINNING

God sent Jesus into the world to invite people to participate once again in God's plan for renewing a marred and disfigured creation. Jesus calls his followers to become a people of God: a network of communities of God's new creation scattered over the world, beginning "in Jerusalem, in all Judea and Samaria, and to the ends of the earth" (Acts 1:8). These communities of Christian disciples are covenant communities called by God to redeem a creation at odds with itself. The purpose of Christian discipleship is to collaborate with God in the risky work of shaping a social sphere in human history that embodies God's original intent for the world and that invites all people to enter, receive, and establish this kingdom.

Called to Live as a New Creation in Christ

I once visited the church built on the site where Jesus supposedly multiplied the loaves and fishes. This church, Tabgha, was built in the fourth century. It is famous for its mosaics that depict birds and fish, plants and animals. These mosaics teem with life and movement. They picture a world transformed and renewed by Jesus' life, death, and resurrection. The early Christian community that worshiped at Tabgha announced God's purposes to the world through these mosaics. Worshipers saw God's new creation all around them—a vision of Paradise renewed.

I once visited the church of San Clemente in Rome. It is a few blocks from the Colosseum, a site that exhibits all Rome's imperial fascination with violence and cruelty. I saw mosaics here too. Above the cross is a tree of life with intertwining leaves and branches representing the leaves of the tree that is for the healing of the nations. Around the leaves and branches are birds and animals and other plants. San Clemente's mosaics also lift worshipers' eyes to a vision of God's new creation. Everywhere worshipers look they are reminded of their mission to be a sign, foretaste, and instrument of God's reign. To be a disciple of Jesus Christ is to share in God's mission to transform creation so that it resembles the renewed Paradise of these early Christian mosaics.

GOD'S REIGN IS NEVER A MATTER OF WORDS ONLY

God's reign must be enfleshed in a real community of men and women. It exists as a social space characterized by collaboration and noncoercive love. It exists as a living, visible community where God's reign is already present, transforming both those who dwell within it and the world around it.

A Demonstration Plot for the Reign of God

I live near the University of Illinois in Champaign-Urbana, which hosts the oldest experimental corn plots in the Western Hemisphere and the second oldest experimental plots in the world—the Morrow Plots. Since 1876, agronomists have been testing seed varieties on these plots. Campus legend says that when the university built its new undergraduate library, architects built it downward into the ground because the university did not want a tall building casting its shadow over the Morrow Plots. Such a change in the pattern of sunlight and shadow would ruin the ability to compare results after the construction of the library with those that go back more than a century.

In Jesus Christ, God calls disciples to be a demonstration plot for God's inbreaking kingdom. God has cultivated this demonstration plot through many generations: Abraham and Sarah, Moses and Elijah, Peter and James, Lydia and Tabitha. The purpose of discipleship is to be a demonstration plot for God's inbreaking kingdom.

One of Jesus' parables compares God's mission to leaven or yeast: "The kingdom of heaven is like yeast that a woman took and mixed in with three measures of flour until all of it was leavened" (Matt. 13:33). Three measures of flour is a significant amount of flour. Yet it takes only a tiny amount of yeast to transform this large quantity of flour into bread. God's reign begins small but becomes unimaginably large. In the same way, God's kingdom begins as something as small and inconsequential as one elderly, childless couple—Abraham and Sarah. It emerges out of something as insignificant as a ragtag group of slaves and refugees fleeing Egypt or a handful of Galilean fishermen. Yet this tiny beginning slowly undermines and overturns the old creation.

The image of "three measures of flour" also echoes the story of Abraham and Sarah. When three visitors came to Abraham's tent at Mamre, he told Sarah to take "three measures of flour" and prepare cakes for them (Gen. 18:6). Jesus' reference to three measures is an echo of the visitor's statement that nothing is impossible for God—not even overturning an old creation damaged by the serpent's seduction.

Matthew's Gospel also tells the parable of the mustard seed. This parable appears immediately before the parable of the leaven: "The kingdom of heaven is like a mustard seed that someone took and sowed in his field; it is the smallest of all the seeds, but when it has grown it is the greatest of shrubs and becomes a tree, so that the birds of the air come and make nests in its branches" (Matt.13:31-32). Mustard plants were an invasive species. They started small but were hard to eradicate. Eventually they would crowd out the other plants, taking over the whole field.

Both parables suggest that God has chosen to restore a broken creation in the smallest, most hidden ways. God starts with us. God invites us to enter and dwell in a concrete, tangible social space called "the reign of God." In this covenant community, God's already present collaborative, noncoercive rule has quietly entered human history. This community announces, invites, and lives with others in ways that erode the old creation's patterns of desire, imitation, rivalry, and violence. Like mustard seeds and leaven, Jesus' followers participate in God's mission to heal a broken world.

Why does Jesus call disciples? He calls disciples to share in the same mission for which God sent him into the world—a mission to reconcile a creation at odds with itself. The purpose of discipleship is to collaborate with God in healing a world spoiled by violence and mired in suspicion and hostility. Those called to this mission embrace a life of noncoercive compassion. They live together as a people called to make their exodus from the old world's hierarchies of power and hoarded goods, of guarded borders and human exploitation.

Disciples of Jesus Christ live together in such a way that God's reign over the world becomes a plausible reality for all people. The visible community of faith within which Jesus' followers dwell is not in and of itself God's kingdom. It is, however, a sign, foretaste, and instrument of God's reign. It is an ever-expanding demonstration plot for God's new creation. It will not look like the original Paradise. But, like the risen Christ's own wounded body, it will bear the scars of its old antagonisms and brutalities now transfigured in love. Daily life in this new community is a discipline of asking how we may more fully welcome and receive God's kingdom into the fabric of our everyday lives both individually and together.

Jesus calls a community of disciples who will do what he did—heal, announce, and teach. As a healing community, the church draws people into God's already present kingdom by demonstrating a love and compassion that overcome a fallen creation's envy, rivalry, hostility, and violence. As a community announcing that God's reign has come near, the church makes a public announcement that God is dwelling in our world right here, right now. As a teaching community, the church apprentices people into an intentional learning of the practices and characteristics possessed by ambassadors of God's reign.

FOR FURTHER REFLECTION

1. If you were to compare your congregation to a demonstration plot for God's reign, what would you point to as the signs of God's kingdom among you?
2. What are some ways you see God's creation disfigured around you by hostility, envy, or violence? What is your congregation doing to respond to these realities?
3. This chapter suggests that the serpent's temptation works first by encouraging a desire to be like someone we admire and whom we therefore want to be like. The desire to possess this person's qualities leads us to envy him or her. Seeing these qualities as scarce goods, we come to see the person we had previously admired as our rival. This rivalry turns to suspicion. And suspicion degenerates into violence. In what ways does this analysis help explain some of the larger conflicts in our nation or world? How does the analysis explain some of the conflicts you experience in the church, home, or workplace?
4. If being a disciple of Jesus Christ means making an exodus out of an old world and living toward a new creation, what are some of the things you need to leave behind or eliminate in your life? In the life of your congregation?
5. What are some ways you see your congregation making a visible, plausible witness to God's reign in your life together?
6. Give some examples of partnership or collaboration in your congregation. What barriers to collaboration exist in your congregation?

7. What difference would it make in your congregation if partici-
    pants thought of God's kingdom as something that is happening
    right now through their collaboration with God? How would
    you and your congregation then make decisions, organize for
    ministry, and live together?

Chapter Two

The Practices of Discipleship

Apprentice, Witness, and Freedom

Jesus repeatedly went against the grain of people's expectations. Israel expected its Messiah to be a politico-military leader, a warrior-king like David who would expel the Romans. Jesus shattered the people's assumptions about who the Messiah would be and how he would save them. Jesus came as a Suffering Servant, a Messiah who suffered on the cross and gave himself to heal a broken creation.

Jesus not only confounded people's expectations about the Messiah; he also exploded their assumptions about God's kingdom. First-century Jewish apocalyptic expectation anticipated that God would defeat sin and evil in a single cataclysmic battle. Jesus instead came proclaiming that God's kingdom had already come near and was now present in his own healing, teaching, and table fellowship. Just as people failed to recognize Jesus as God's Messiah, they failed to comprehend his announcement that God's reign was near.

According to Jesus, God's kingdom is not a reality outside time and history that will come sometime in the distant future. Nor does God's kingdom arrive in one cataclysmic moment. Instead, God has already begun to rule over the world. God is working patiently to unfold this present but hidden kingdom in human history.

God's reign is something easily overlooked, like a little leaven in a barrel of flour or a few mustard seeds in a field. Despite its hidden character, people can choose to recognize God's kingdom, receive it, and enter into it—right here, right now. God's reign is not coming from the clouds. It comes in history as people choose to live as part of God's new creation: "For where two or three are gathered in my name, I am there among them" (Matt. 18:20). By receiving and dwelling in God's kingdom, Jesus' followers make it visible and plausible here and now.

Those who dwell under God's rule are not conformed to the pattern of this world. They live and interact with the world in distinctive ways (Rom. 12:2). Three specific words express this way of life: *apprenticeship*, *witness*, and *freedom*. They are like three facets of a multifaceted diamond. Each reveals an important attribute of discipleship.

MATTHEW'S GOSPEL: DISCIPLES AS THOSE APPRENTICED TO JESUS

The word *disciple* occurs about 270 times in the New Testament, but authors vary in the frequency with which they use this word. Paul rarely uses the word *disciple*. Matthew, on the other hand, uses it more than 70 times, compared to its occurrence about 45 times in Mark and 35 times in Luke. As you can see, Matthew employs the word *disciple* almost twice as often as Mark and Luke combined.

Disciples as Students and Learners

The Greek word we translate as "disciple" (*mathetes*) literally means "learner." It derives from the Greek verb for "to learn." Matthew portrays Jesus as a teacher and his disciples as learners or pupils.

Disciples are scribes who have learned Jesus' interpretation of God's commandments. They are the ones Jesus has trained for the kingdom of God. They bring forth this wisdom wherever and whenever needed: "Every scribe who has been trained for the kingdom of heaven is like the master of a household who brings out of his treasure what is new and what is old" (Matt. 13:52).

Matthew's Gospel adopts Mark's basic outline of Jesus' life, but he then inserts large blocks of teaching material: the Sermon on the Mount (chap. 5–7); the missionary discourse (chap. 10); the discourse on parables (chap. 13); the discourse on church order (chap. 18); and the discourse on the coming kingdom (chap. 24–25). Matthew intends for this teaching material to be used in training scribes "for the kingdom of heaven" (13:52).

Matthew's emphasis on knowing scripture also appears in his extensive use of quotations from the Hebrew scriptures. Matthew's Gospel quotes from the Hebrew scriptures more than ten times. He begins by saying, "All this took place to fulfill what had been spoken by the Lord through the prophet" (1:22). He then proceeds to narrate events in Jesus' life that fulfill the prophecies (1:23-25; 2:15, 17-18; 4:14-16; 8:17; 12:17-21; 13:35; 21:5; 27:9-10). By adopting this pattern, Matthew is modeling how scribes trained for the kingdom of heaven draw upon their knowledge of scripture to proclaim the gospel.

The Disciple as an Apprentice Who Learns by Doing

Matthew's Jesus is also highly critical of scribes and their learning. This criticism is not directed at scribal knowledge itself. Jesus criticizes the scribes and Pharisees because they do not practice what they preach. Matthew's Gospel distinguishes between people who see Jesus only as a teacher from whom they can learn and those who see him as a Lord whom they should follow. In Matthew,

Jesus' opponents and those who turn away from him address him as "Teacher." His disciples and those whom he heals or redeems, on the other hand, almost never address him this way. Instead, they call him "Lord." Disciples are more than learners who need a teacher. They are believers who need a Lord.

Significantly, Matthew seldom uses the verb for "to learn," although Jesus' disciples are "learners." The verb for "to learn" occurs only three times in Matthew. Matthew instead uses the Greek word for "to follow" (*akolouthein*). A disciple "follows" or "walks" in Jesus' way. Jesus' disciples are followers who learn by observing and doing what Jesus does.

This pattern mirrors Israel's covenant traditions. The Hebrew scriptures frequently speak of following or walking (*hlk*) in God's ways. As Moses tells Israel in Deuteronomy 5:32-33: "You must therefore be careful to do as the LORD your God has commanded you; you shall not turn to the right or to the left. You must follow [*hlk*] exactly the path that the LORD your God has commanded you, so that you may live, and that it may go well with you." Abraham's faithfulness arose from his walking [*hlk*] in God's presence. "The LORD appeared to Abram, and said to him, 'I am God Almighty, walk [*hlk*] in my presence, and be blameless'" (Gen. 17:1; my translation). When Elijah calls Elisha as his successor, Elisha says, "Let me kiss my father and my mother, and then I will follow [*hlk 'hr*] you" (1 Kings 19:20). To be a disciple is not only to believe or understand, it is to practice a specific way of life.

According to Matthew, faith is an action we take, not a belief we express: "Not everyone who says to me, 'Lord, Lord,' will enter the kingdom of heaven, but only the one who does the will of my Father in heaven" (7:21). Matthew's emphasis on active doing accounts for his addition of the phrase "Your will be done" to the

Lord's Prayer, a phrase that is missing in Luke's version (Matt. 6:10; Luke 11:2). Matthew is also the only Gospel that includes the parable of the two sons (Matt. 21:28-30). One son promises his father that he will go to the vineyard, but then he never shows up. The other son refuses his father's request, but he later comes to the vineyard and does what his father asked of him. According to Jesus, the faithful son is not the one who makes an empty promise. The faithful son is the one who does what God requires.

We are not disciples of Jesus Christ because we have accumulated information about God, Jesus, or the Bible. According to Matthew, we are disciples when we walk with Jesus to the cross. Following Jesus is not primarily a matter of knowledge and information. It is a specific way of living—a set of practices—through which we embody the gospel in our own lives as part of a community of people who have made the same commitment to walk in Jesus' path.

A more accurate translation of the word *disciple* might be "apprentice." An apprentice is also a learner, and apprenticeship suggests we learn by doing. A novice is apprenticed to a master worker and learns by conversation, observation, and—most important of all— by working alongside someone with a set of skills the novice wishes to learn and adopt.

Describing discipleship in terms of an apprenticeship to Jesus encourages us to see in a new light his invitation to take his yoke upon us (Matt. 11:28-30). Oxen are yoked in order to pull, to plow, to carry, to work. When we are yoked to Christ, we are apprenticed to do the work for which God sent Christ into the world: to fulfill God's mission of transfiguring our world so that it becomes once more the good creation God intended. Jesus prayed for his enemies. He did not respond to violence with violence. He spoke truthfully. He refused to covet what belonged to others, and he loved both God and neighbor. Jesus embodied what God intended human life to be before the serpent's introduction of desire, envy, rivalry, and violence. His disciples are apprentices who learn how to align their lives with Jesus' own cross-shaped life.

God's Reign as Personal Experience and Social Reality

Disciples as apprentices means envisioning discipleship as a collaborative rather than a personal project. Apprenticeships are partnerships in learning and transformation. An apprentice learns by following, observing, and rehearsing new performances alongside others who have already walked the same path and know its pitfalls and possibilities. There are things I cannot discover on my own. I learn them only as I work side by side with others. Jesus did not send out solitary evangelists and missionaries. He sent them forth in pairs. They traveled and worked together.

Matthew's Gospel not only gives priority to action over belief but emphasizes the social and communal aspects of discipleship. For Matthew, walking Jesus' cross-shaped path is something we always do together. His instructions on church order arise out of this concern for the social aspect of faith. Matthew gives careful attention to how church conflict is handled. If God's original creation was wrecked by the serpent's introduction of suspicion, hostility, and conflict among people, then how the church handles this suspicion, hostility, and conflict becomes critical to its embodiment of God's new creation. Conflict is not just a personal matter between individuals. It compromises the church's witness to God's reign.

Faithful living always includes a social, communal dimension. God's kingdom is not just a personal kingdom that comes into our hearts. It is also a social reality that comes into our world through the church's shared life and witness.

Apprenticed into Generosity

Matthew's Gospel gives special emphasis to concrete social practices like generosity and almsgiving. Along with fasting and prayer, generosity is an essential dimension of the spiritual life (Matt. 6:1-8). Generosity breaks the serpent's cycle of desire, envy, and greed. It empowers us to release our possessions rather than cling jealously to them. Generosity thus signifies the presence of God's reign among us.

In Matthew 20:1-16, Jesus tells the parable of the laborers in the vineyard. A landowner contracts with various workers throughout the day to work in his vineyard. At the end of the day, he pays the same wage to all workers regardless of when their workday started. Those hired in the early morning grumble about their compensation, to which the landowner responds, "Am I not allowed to do what I choose with what belongs to me? Or are you envious because I am generous?" (Matt. 20:15). The parable contrasts envy and generosity. Envy and generosity represent the core values of two very different worlds. They also produce two distinct sets of social relationships. Envy presupposes the serpent's world of scarcity, desire, greed, and rivalry. Generosity assumes an abundant creation. Such abundance is a fundamental characteristic of God's original creation. When people respond to others with generosity and openness, God's reign has come near as a social reality among us.

Apprenticed into Hospitality

Generosity is not the only practice that points toward the abundance of God's reign. Like generosity, hospitality is a sign of God's abundance. God generously welcomes us into a good creation filled with abundance.

Jesus' ministry is characterized by acts of welcoming, particularly to table fellowship with him. Shared meals are a primary way we establish social relationships. What we eat and with whom we eat are reflective of our social system. Before desegregation in the United States, prohibitions on who could eat where and with whom provided a dramatic example of how meals reflected and reinforced our social system. In a peasant society characterized by purity rules that excluded the hungry poor, Jesus invited the marginal, the outcast, and the invisible to share meals with him: "The Son of Man came eating and drinking, and they say, 'Look, a glutton and a drunkard, a friend of tax collectors and sinners!'" (Matt. 11:19).

When Jesus welcomed outcasts to table fellowship, what appeared to be scarcity disclosed a hidden abundance. Although the disciples could find only five loaves and two fish, they fed a crowd of more than five thousand people and then picked up twelve baskets of leftovers (Matt. 14:13-21). Abundance characterizes the kingdom of God. Thus the petition for bread in the Lord's Prayer immediately follows the petition for God's kingdom. When bread is broken and strangers are welcomed, God's reign is established on earth as it is in heaven.

Generosity and hospitality are practices that characterize the abundance of God's reign. They are visible signs of God's kingdom. Rooted in Jesus' own acts of table fellowship and healing, these practices relativize all the ways we derive our personal and social identities from comparison and competition.

Apprenticed into Service and Outreach

Jesus' shared meals were not just occasions of hospitality and generous abundance. They were also acts of service and outreach. First-century Galilee was a peasant society under considerable economic and social stress. The vast majority of its inhabitants lived a subsistence existence. Most people were hungry on a daily basis. Shared meals were not just spiritual gatherings. On these occasions those who were truly hungry received real food and drink. Hospitality and generosity therefore were specific responses to the people's physical hungers and hurts. By sharing meals with one another and the hungry, Jesus and his disciples were serving others and meeting human needs.

Service to others represents another concrete practice through which disciples of Jesus Christ make visible God's reign. Jesus told his followers, "You know that the rulers of the Gentiles lord it over them, and their great ones are tyrants over them. It will not be so among you; but whoever wishes to be great among you must be your servant, and whoever wishes to be first among you must be your slave; just as the Son of Man came not to be served but to serve, and to give his life a ransom for many" (Matt. 20:25-28).

When we are apprenticed to Jesus, we practice a life of service and outreach. When the naked are clothed, the sick receive care, the hungry are fed, and the thirsty given a drink, God's reign comes near (Matt. 25:31-46). This humble service stands in sharp contrast to the values of a fallen creation. The serpent's triumph in the Garden creates a social world of comparison and competition. Rivalry and envy are the ultimate consequences of comparing ourselves to others. When we set ourselves above others or claim special status for ourselves, we sow the seeds of envy and rivalry, of hostility and violence.

Serving others reverses this fascination with competition, status, and personal power. We attend to the needs of others because we know they share a common humanity with us. When one suffers, we all suffer. When one is hungry or thirsty, we are all hungry and thirsty. Humble service is a visible demonstration that others are "bone of my bone and flesh of my flesh," as God originally created us to be (Gen. 2:23). Serving others restores the common social bond that existed before the serpent's curse of suspicion and hostility took root among us.

Apprenticed to Jesus as Partners in God's Mission

Matthew's emphasis on discipleship allows us to see an important facet of what it means to follow Jesus: A disciple is someone who has been apprenticed to Jesus and walks in Jesus' way. Jesus calls disciples to take his yoke upon them and learn from him. But this is not an abstract learning of facts and concepts and dogmas. It is learning by doing. It is also not just a personal walk with Jesus. We are yoked with Jesus as part of a community of his followers. Together we form a concrete social space where God's reign is embodied, however partially and imperfectly.

Through our participation in the church, we are informed, formed, and transformed as apprentices to Jesus for the sake of God's reign in the world. As a people informed by the church, we are active learners who seek to understand the faith, think for ourselves, and choose to live in a new way. As a people apprenticed to Jesus, we are formed in community for a whole way of life. Jesus calls us to a lifelong process of transformation. Those apprenticed to Jesus are engaged in an ongoing conversion of the heart and mind.

JOHN'S GOSPEL: A COMMUNITY OF WITNESSES

Matthew's Gospel describes Jesus' followers as apprentices who are schooled in practices of generosity and hospitality, service and outreach. John's Gospel, on the other hand, does not privilege the word *disciple* as a description of Jesus' followers. The Gospel of John instead uses a different term that illuminates another facet of discipleship.

Discipleship as Testimony and Witness

The verb for "to witness" occurs thirty-plus times in John's Gospel and ten times in John's letters. The synoptic Gospels, on the other hand, almost never use this verb. Similarly, the noun *witness* appears nearly fifteen times in John's Gospel. It occurs about seven times in John's letters and nine times in the book of Revelation. The rest of the New Testament uses *witness* fewer than ten times. "Witness" is therefore a distinctive, fundamental way through which John's community understands what it means to follow Jesus. It points to a different emphasis than what we find in Matthew's Gospel.

The Spirit of Truth and Our Witness to God's Reign

On the night he was betrayed, Jesus promised his followers that "when the Advocate comes, whom I will send to you from the Father, the Spirit of truth who comes from the Father, he will testify on my behalf. You also are to testify because you have been with me from the beginning" (John 15:26-27). According to John, the primary task of Jesus' disciples is to witness or testify to God's mission as revealed in the life, death, and resurrection of Jesus Christ. This is not a task the disciples accomplish on their own. Their witness is made possible by the gift of the "Paraclete," or the Spirit of truth. It has already testified to who Jesus is and now empowers his followers to bear witness to what they have seen, heard, and touched as his disciples.

John uses the Greek word *Paraclete* to describe this Spirit of truth. *Paraclete* is possibly a legal term that refers to an attorney who comes alongside someone and speaks on his or her behalf. Like witness and testimony, *Paraclete* is drawn from the language of courts and legal proceedings. Courtroom witnesses must tell the truth—the whole truth and nothing but the truth. They tell the truth of what they have seen, heard, and experienced. This is precisely what Jesus' followers do when they receive the Spirit of truth: "We declare to you what was from the beginning, what we have heard, what we have seen with our eyes, what we have looked at and touched with our hands, concerning the word of life—this life was revealed, and we have seen it and testify to it" (1 John 1:1-2). The Paraclete is the Spirit of truth because it empowers a testimony or witness that is true to the disciples' experience of Jesus. Their witness makes God's kingdom visible and plausible to others.

In John 1:38-39, two of John the Baptizer's disciples come to Jesus and ask where he is "staying." Jesus turns and says to them, "Come and see." The Greek word used here for "staying" can also be translated as "abide" or "dwell." This is one of John's favorite words—it occurs almost forty times in the Gospel of John, compared to twelve times in the other three Gospels combined. Jesus comes as the Light of the world, and those who abide in him no longer abide in the darkness of a wrecked creation (John 12:46). He tells his followers to abide in him the way the branch abides in the vine, which will allow them to bear much fruit (John 15:4-5). To abide in Jesus is to receive, enter into, and dwell within God's reign. Jesus' followers dwell or abide in a new social space that bears good fruit, not the corrupting fruit the serpent offered to the first man and woman.

Disciples of Jesus Christ are witnesses to this new creation in Jesus Christ—a new creation where God's rule has already taken root and, like leaven or a mustard seed, is slowly transforming a fallen world. Disciples pay attention to their own personal experiences of what it is like to live within the reign of God. Their testimonies emerge out of this attention to their own inner experiences. Such testimonies require thoughtful discernment of the Spirit through the Paraclete's guidance and direction.

We live so much of our lives on the surface. Constant noise, distraction, and interruption tempt us to focus on the superficial. The demands of work and family and the incessant busyness of our lives squeeze out any time to reflect and to discern. Traditional spiritual disciplines such as a daily examination of conscience or keeping a journal combat this anesthetizing of our lives. They connect us back to our own experiences, allowing us to discern where God's spirit is at work. Sabbath is not meant as a day to "catch up" on all the things we could not complete during the other six days. It is intended for refreshment and renewal. It is meant to be an experience of the world as God originally intended it, before it became marred and disfigured.

To discern in our own experiences the presence of God's kingdom requires disciplined attention to the life of the Spirit. This attention is possible because the Spirit of truth dwells in us and we dwell in it (John 14:16-17). The practice of spiritual disciplines increases our capacity to be open and available to the Spirit of truth. Spiritual disciplines are not methods to enrich our personal lives or to improve our mental and physical well-being. They are ways to increase our capacity to discern where and how God's reign is at work within us, around us, and among us. We share the fruit of this discernment in testimony and witness.

Personal Witness Grounded in the Biblical Witness

If God's reign is spread over the earth but humanity does not perceive it, our task is to testify to its visible, plausible presence among us here and now. Our testimonies to what we have heard, seen, and touched challenge listeners to examine their own lives for similar signs of God's kingdom. A witness's testimony always tells a story that is true to her or his own experience. This testimony simultaneously invites listeners to discover truth in their own lives.

Testimony is more than a recitation of our own experiences. It relates our personal experiences to a long tradition of faithfulness to God. As a people educated in the spiritual wisdom of the Christian tradition—its scriptures, creeds, ethics, ways of worship, and words of prayer—we receive the tools to interpret our own experience in more discerning ways. This was the dynamic of Paul's testimony to what the Spirit was doing among Gentile congregations when he and Barnabas appeared before the Jerusalem Council (Acts 15). Council members used the biblical story to interpret Paul and Barnabas's story, and their testimonies invited council members to embrace a new understanding of it. Paul, Barnabas, and the members of the council draw upon their personal experiences to interpret scripture in fresh ways, and they find new meaning in their personal experiences by examining them in light of scripture. Learning to tell one's personal testimony cannot be separated from knowing the biblical story deeply.

Serious problems with personal testimony arise when either the biblical or the personal story is neglected. The church sometimes tells the biblical story in such a distant, conceptual way that people cannot identify with it. They are left with the impression that God's mission is merely an abstract idea. It is never fleshed out in human testimony that points to its reality here and now in a particular community of people. Testimony might also err when it is so focused on the individual's story that it functionally eliminates God from the narrative. Such testimony reduces God to a minor actor in what becomes the drama of the individual's own heroic story of personal transformation. Testimony thus ceases to be framed within the story of God's larger purposes. Faithful testimony always holds a witness's personal story and God's story in creative tension with each other.

Testimony That Listens as Well as Speaks

"Witness" is also a collaborative term. According to Jewish law, it takes at least two witnesses to confirm the truth (Deut. 19:15). Likewise, legal testimony is usually given in person. Witnesses speak in the presence of others. Testimony ties the individual to the community because speaking cannot be separated from listening. As we grow in our ability to listen to our own experiences, we also mature in our capacity to listen to others as they describe their experiences of God. Listening for God in our own experiences trains us to listen for God in what others are saying about their experiences of God.

The testimony of others can enrich our own perspectives. This often means that we must be open to the witness of people whose experiences of God are very different from our own. We need to listen to others in order to better understand our own faith. Learning to listen to others' testimonies enriches our own experiences of God and makes us better witnesses.

Paul and Freedom in Christ

Paul uses neither the word *disciple* nor the word *witness* to describe what it means to follow Jesus. Instead, he uses yet another term, which provides a third glimpse into the multifaceted diamond we call discipleship—freedom. The words *freedom*, *free*, and *freed* occur almost forty times in Paul's letters. Freedom is a key concept in Paul's understanding of what it means to follow Jesus.

FREEDOM IN CHRIST JESUS

Paul's understanding of Christian freedom was grounded in Jesus' own freedom. To follow Jesus is to walk in the same freedom that characterized his life and ministry. The overwhelming characteristic of Jesus is his freedom. His interpretation of the Torah is free from a restrictive traditional reading: "You have heard it said . . . But I say to you . . ." (Matt. 5:21-22, 27-28, 31-32, 33-34, 38-39, 43-44). While a faithful child of his parents, Luke describes Jesus as free from the claims of family (Luke 11:27-28). Jesus calls his followers to be free from concerns about clothes and shelter (Matt. 6:25-34). This freedom is not for its own sake. It is for the sake of others. Jesus is free to be compassionate toward others because he is free from worry about himself (Mark 10:42-44).

Jesus' freedom is contagious because it has the power to set others free from enslavement and alienation. To be "in Christ" is to understand oneself as free, to be a new creation where the old patterns of desire, rivalry, and violence no longer rule. Freedom characterizes God's reign because God's kingdom is not established or maintained through coercion and control.

Those who follow Jesus are "in Christ" and are free from the tendency to rely on their own moral and religious achievements to justify themselves (Gal. 2:15-21). Following Jesus means being free from the coercion of others who want to regulate your life according to a moral or legal code that is imposed rather than chosen (Rom. 7:4-6). Those who are in Christ are free from the bonds of death and all that deals death, including the competition and competitiveness that lead to hostility and violence (Rom. 8:21, 38-39). Followers of Jesus are free from the fear that made the first man and the first woman hide themselves from each other and from God (Rom. 8:15-18; Gal. 4:1-7). They are free from the fear of other people's judgments and from the cycle of desire and imitation that engenders rivalry and coercive manipulation (1 Cor. 3:17-18). Most importantly, Christians are given this freedom not in order to be free *from* others but to be free *for* others. They are free to give themselves in love to their neighbors and even to their enemies (1 Cor. 9:19; 1 Thess. 2:8). Thus, Paul's concept of freedom is intimately related to his ethic of love (1 Cor. 13).

PRACTICES OF DISCIPLESHIP

Matthew's emphasis on apprenticeship, John's focus on witness and testimony, and Paul's highlighting of freedom provide a robust and comprehensive picture of discipleship. Our survey of Matthew, John, and Paul has identified at least six basic practices that characterize disciples of Jesus Christ. While these six practices are listed separately, they are not separate practices. Each reinforces and supports the others. Practicing one leads to growth in the others. Neglect of one practice weakens the others.

Knowing and Living Scripture

Jesus' disciples are always growing in their knowledge of scripture. Biblical literacy includes knowing how to find the books of the Old and the New Testaments. Disciples can retell basic biblical stories in their own words.

As we grow familiar with the Bible, we gradually begin to recognize overarching themes, symbols, and metaphors. A simple symbol like the tree appears in Genesis as the tree of life, reappears in the Gospels as the tree upon which Jesus is crucified, and then occurs in the last pages of Revelation as the tree whose leaves are for the healing of the nations. Themes like creation, covenant, election, call, grace, and discipleship are interwoven throughout the whole Bible. A biblically literate disciple recognizes these themes and makes connections among them.

Disciples of Jesus Christ understand how the Bible came to take its current shape and form. The Bible has a history. Knowing this history, and our ability to answer the following questions, is an important part of biblical literacy: Who decided what books would constitute various components of the Bible? What historical events shaped the collection of these materials into their present form? To understand this history we must also be able to identify the Bible's various literary styles and how each makes a unique contribution to our faith formation.

Biblical literacy cannot be attained without a solid familiarity with commentaries, atlases, and concordances. Knowing where to find these tools and how to use them is essential to our growth as disciples.

Another dimension of biblical literacy includes knowing how to lead others in studying the Bible. Faithful teaching of the Bible includes formational and transformational approaches to scripture such as *lectio divina* and the African Bible Study.

Biblical literacy ultimately culminates in the ability to speak personally about how the Bible addresses our own lives. Studying the Bible is not an intellectual exercise. It is not about learning facts and dates or memorizing chapters and verses. The goal is to do all

Jesus commanded (Matt. 28:20), and to testify to God's reign by linking our stories to the larger biblical story.

Practicing Spiritual Disciplines

Jesus' followers practice the classic Christian spiritual disciplines. Whatever their life stage or personality, disciples need strategies for adopting and practicing a spiritual discipline or disciplines on a consistent basis so they are continually opening themselves up to new freedom in Christ. Spiritual disciplines prepare our hearts to receive God's spirit, which sets us free from negative social and personal patterns that bind us to the old creation. Spiritual disciplines open a space within us where the Spirit of truth and freedom can work, releasing us from whatever binds us to a fallen creation's temptation, rivalry and envy, coercion and violence.

Disciples of Jesus Christ can name and describe various personal and corporate spiritual disciplines. They have the ability to explain the relationship between these disciplines and particular phases of life or personal temperaments. Not all disciplines are a good fit for every personality or temperament. Likewise, a disciple may go through a particular phase of life where some disciplines are a better match than others for his or her situation.

Disciples know how to locate resources that help in the practice of the spiritual disciplines. They know where to find devotional guides for themselves or others. They are able to interpret different spiritual disciplines and understand how to adapt them for different personalities or life situations.

Growing in our practice of spiritual disciplines means growing in our awareness of important spiritual or devotional writers in the Christian tradition and how their testimony can inform, form, and transform our own testimonies to God's mission to heal a broken world.

Practicing Hospitality and Generosity

Disciples literate in the Bible know its stories of hospitality and generosity. They use these stories to interpret the needs of others around them and respond appropriately. They testify to how they themselves have received the generosity and hospitality of others. Disciples are free from a fallen creation's compulsion to see others as hostile rivals in a world of scarcity. Consequently, they are free to live their lives for God and others.

Practicing Service and Outreach

Disciples do not just say, "Lord, Lord." They are free to make a visible and plausible witness to God's mission of a new heaven and new earth. Disciples are doers of the faith. Consequently, they are able to name the spiritual gifts for ministry identified in the Bible and name their own personal spiritual gifts for service and outreach.

Disciples know how to discern opportunities for service to individuals. Apprenticed to a Jesus who gives himself freely for others, they give of themselves in service and outreach. They also know that personal righteousness and social justice are two sides of our experience of God's reign. They therefore seek ways to address and be advocates for societal and global issues.

Discerning Our Experience of God

Disciples of Jesus Christ are able to reflect on their own experiences in light of their faith and to discern God's presence, power, and purposes in their lives. They practice spiritual disciplines that help them discern experiences of God's presence. This capacity grows as they learn the vocabulary of scripture and tradition for discernment and listening to the movement of God in one's life. For this reason, they are familiar with how devotional and spiritual writers throughout Christian history have described the process of discerning our experiences of God.

Disciples easily identify the sources that influence their faith. These sources include the four components of the Wesleyan quadrilateral: scripture, tradition, reason, and experience. Disciples work to understand how these four sources may take on different emphases during an individual's life span.

Testifying to Our Experience of God

As one's faith deepens, the call to testify to what God is doing in one's life also deepens. Disciples are able and willing to speak with others about their own experiences of God and share their testimonies with others individually and in groups.

Witness is not limited to speaking, however. Growing in our capacity to listen to the faith experiences of others—particularly those whose articulation of their faith is different from our own—is also an expression of Christian witness. By their capacity to listen, disciples draw others to reflect more deeply on their own experiences. As disciples open themselves to the testimonies of others, they broaden their appreciation for how God works in people's lives and in the world.

FOR FURTHER REFLECTION

1. This chapter highlights three words that describe Jesus' followers: *apprenticeship*, *witness*, and *freedom*. Which of these three words speaks most powerfully to you? What makes the word's meaning appealing to you?

2. In what ways does the description of a disciple as an apprentice enrich your understanding of what it means to follow Jesus?

3. Read these passages and summarize what they say about discipleship: Matthew 7:21-23; 13:24-30, 47-50; 21:28-32; 25:1-46.

4. What are some ways your own discipleship includes acts of service, hospitality, and generosity?

5. How does the theme of discipleship as testimony or witness challenge you?

6. Read and reflect on these passages from Paul's letters: 1 Corinthians 7:21-22; 9:19; 2 Corinthians 3:17; Galatians 5:1. What do you think Paul means by "freedom"? From what in your life do you need to be made free? Where is there evidence of your being "free for others" in your life?

7. Looking at the characteristics of a disciple in the chart on the next page, how do you embody each characteristic? What steps might you take to grow as a disciple of Jesus Christ?

FIGURE 2.1

Characteristic	How do I now embody this characteristic?	What needs to happen for more of this characteristic to show up in my discipleship?
Knowing and living scripture		
Hospitality and generosity		
Service and outreach		
Practicing spiritual disciplines		
Discerning experiences of God in myself and in the world		
Witnessing to the presence, power, and purpose of God in my life		

CHAPTER THREE

THE STAGES OF DISCIPLESHIP

The human body is composed of trillions of cells. These cells are continuously dying and being replaced. Red blood cells live about four months. Skin cells survive approximately one month. Despite the body's constant physical transformation, we wake up each morning feeling that we are the same person we were the night before. People are not like snakes that shed their skins all at once. Our physical bodies are changing continuously, but this transformation is so pervasive and constant that we are hardly aware it is happening. Only when we undergo major surgery or suffer a serious illness do we suddenly become aware of physical changes in our bodies.

Our inner sense of self is likewise constantly changing. Each day we encounter people and situations that leave their imprint on us. Some experiences enrich our lives. Others wound us. None leave us unchanged. Some changes happen quietly and unconsciously. Others are intentional decisions we make in response to events or people around us.

Our discipleship undergoes a similar process of transformation. It evolves over time, just like the human body or our sense of self. Each day's encounters leave their imprints on how we think and act. Our experiences change us—sometimes quietly and imperceptibly, sometimes visibly and dramatically. Discipleship is not a steady state where, once we reach a certain point, we cease to grow in our love, knowledge, and service of God and neighbor. We are always becoming disciples of Jesus Christ.

DISCIPLESHIP AS A PILGRIM'S JOURNEY

This process of continuous change and transformation is why the image of a journey or pilgrimage remains such a common metaphor for following Jesus. People still read John Bunyan's *The Pilgrim's Progress* for its description of the Christian life as a journey to God. The Gospels and the book of Acts often use the Greek word for "road" or "way" to characterize what it means to follow Jesus (Acts 9:2). Even in an age of bullet trains and jet planes, describing discipleship as a journey resonates with Christians. We are conscious and intentional about some steps along this journey. Others happen below the surface of our awareness. To be a disciple of Jesus Christ is to be a pilgrim who walks a particular spiritual path. The more we understand this path, the better equipped we are to grow as disciples and to help others grow.

The Labyrinth: Outward Pilgrimage and Inward Journey

Christians sometimes travel as pilgrims to holy places. These outward, physical journeys can prompt personal insights into our inner, spiritual journeys. Not everyone has the time or resources to make an actual physical pilgrimage. Many churches therefore have recovered an ancient spiritual practice that uses an outward, physical walk to spark insights into one's own inner journey. During Lent, our congregation sometimes lays out a labyrinth in our social hall. People walk this labyrinth as part of their Lenten spiritual practice. As we walk the labyrinth, we better understand the inner journey of Christian discipleship.

The stages of discipleship defy easy categorization. When looked at from above, the labyrinth appears as a circle divided into four quadrants. These four sections often represent the four stages of life: childhood, adolescence, adulthood, and aging. They might also symbolize four stages of discipleship: inquiry, call, growth, and maturity in Christ. We do not walk the labyrinth sequentially, going from the first quadrant to the second and then to the next one. The labyrinth is full of hairpin turns. The path curves back into earlier quadrants as it advances toward its goal.

The human life span also tends to double back upon itself. Each stage of life contains and prefigures all the others. A small child still lives inside the oldest adult, and children can possess a wisdom that eludes their grandparents. In the same way, each stage of discipleship includes and anticipates the others. Disciples carry the imprints of prior stages into later ones. Characteristics of advanced stages can first appear in earlier ones. Growth as a disciple of Jesus Christ is never a strictly linear process. It is more a spiral than a straight line. We keep spiraling back to earlier stages, revisiting certain prior practices and choices as we move forward.

Two conclusions can be drawn from walking a labyrinth. First, we need to exercise caution in categorizing people according to their apparent stage of discipleship. The most important distinction is not between one stage of discipleship and another. What matters most is that all followers of Jesus Christ are on the same path. We can learn from and support one another regardless of where we find ourselves on the journey. Just because people are new disciples does not mean they lack insights to share with others who have been on the path for a long time. In the same way, just because someone has been on the path for a long time does not mean she or he is exempt from the struggles of an earlier stage. Walking the labyrinth teaches us to exercise nonjudgmental openness toward all disciples, practicing hospitality and generosity. Discipleship presupposes listening with discernment to the experiences of others, regardless of how new or how seasoned they may be.

Second, the spiral character of our pilgrimage means that we build our capacity to navigate future stages by carefully listening to our present experiences as disciples. We progress in our discipleship by paying attention to our own experiences as well as learning from others and from the larger Christian tradition's voices of experience. We are not the first to have walked this path, and we can learn from those who have gone before us.

The path and the goal are one. A six-petaled center lies at the heart of our labyrinth. A single pathway leads pilgrims from the labyrinth's entrance to this center. Both the path and the center are outlined in the same color. In other words, the path itself is a visual extension of the center. Or, depending on your point of view, the center is an extension of the path. As disciples of Jesus Christ, our destination and our path are not two separate realities. They are two aspects of the same reality. Jesus Christ is the goal and the path and the guide along the way.

In Luke's story of Jesus' encounter with two disciples on the Emmaus road, the two disciples meet a stranger (24:13-35). Although they do not recognize him, this stranger is the risen Christ. Along the road, the disciples and the stranger they have encountered interpret the scriptures and share their reactions to the week's events in Jerusalem. Later, when the stranger blesses and breaks bread at their evening meal, the two disciples recognize him as the risen Christ. If they had not spent time walking and talking together, would the disciples have recognized the stranger as the Risen One? Was their recognition of Jesus at the journey's end the natural extension of the conversation they had shared along the way? Which is the goal and which is the path? Luke's story illuminates how the journey and the destination are two sides of one experience. Dwelling in God's kingdom and following Jesus into the kingdom are not two separate experiences. They are two ways of experiencing the same reality. If we neglect the path, we miss the goal.

The journey is away from comparison and competition. I have seen some people speed through a labyrinth. They hurry to reach the center and rush back out. The labyrinth is not a NASCAR race. Growth as a disciple of Jesus Christ cannot be rushed. Ultimately, growth depends less on us than on God's grace. The practices of discipleship prepare the soil of our lives to receive God's spirit. But discipleship is not something we can rush and hurry and make happen all on our own.

The most effective way to hinder our growth as disciples is to spend too much time evaluating whether we are growing as fast as possible. Seeing discipleship as a series of stages can inadvertently encourage such thinking. I sometimes plant my garden seeds too early in the spring. The weather turns cold and the seeds lie in cold, damp soil. I start to worry whether they are still alive. So I anxiously dig them up and check on their growth. By digging them up, however, I pull apart their tiny roots and make it impossible for them to survive. In the same way, when we worry too much about our stage of growth, we harm rather than help our development as disciples of Jesus Christ.

I am not in a race with others to see how quickly I can finish. The labyrinth's turns and multiple circuits make it impossible to compare one pilgrim's progress to another's. As I walk the path, some pilgrims seem to be closer to the center than I am. Later I look again, and they appear behind me. The labyrinth is a set of circuits we traverse. It is not a ladder we climb. Along the path of discipleship, we cannot always tell who is thoroughly seasoned and who is just beginning.

One danger inherent in every stage theory of human development is that they encourage us to compare and compete. We pigeonhole people, describing them in terms of stages ahead or behind us. We compare ourselves to others, and we no longer experience others as companions but as competitors. These habits of competition and rivalry are part and parcel of a game the serpent has been playing since seducing the first man and woman in the Garden. Jesus calls us to leave this game behind us and to enter a new way of life characterized by inclusion and partnership. Discipleship is meant to be a visible, living demonstration of God's reign where competition, rivalry, and envy have been conquered.

All stages of discipleship include intentional spiritual practices. A group of us once entered the labyrinth together. A few minutes into the experience, I realized one member was exiting the path. She stepped out of the labyrinth with a puzzled look on her face. Later I asked her what had happened. She said she was not watching the path, but rather her eyes were following the footsteps of the person ahead of her. When the path made one of its turns, she took her eyes off his feet and accidentally focused on someone else's feet—only this person was exiting the labyrinth. Following these other footsteps, she found herself walking in the other direction.

Her story explains why all six discipleship practices described in chapter 2 are critical to growing in the love, knowledge, and service of God and neighbor. We need all six practices to help us keep our eyes on Jesus and follow where he leads. These six discipleship practices are woven into all stages of following Jesus. We will not grow as disciples without engaging in them.

The Risks and Benefits of Stage Theories of Discipleship

Stage theories of discipleship carry both risks and benefits. They can oversimplify the complexity of our lives. They may imply a natural unfolding of stages that is effortless or suggest that growth happens without disciplined practice. They easily deceive us into thinking we are finished with particular issues because we have passed beyond a certain stage. They can encourage us to stereotype people. The linear nature of stage models might unwittingly promote comparing ourselves to others and thus engender a subtle form of spiritual competition.

On the other hand, stage models encourage us to think critically about what we need to grow. Stages models can be especially helpful to church leaders responsible for creating and overseeing a congregation's discipleship system. They assist leaders in assessing a congregation's current discipleship system. They help leaders identify gaps in this system as well as unidentified barriers that are limiting people's development as disciples.

STAGES ALONG THE WAY OF DISCIPLESHIP

In Jesus' parable of the sower, God is described as a farmer who casts seeds everywhere. Some seeds fall on hard soil and birds carry them away. Others fall into thin soil and die after sprouting. Weeds choke out other seeds. Still others fall on well-prepared soil and produce abundant results. If the church is a demonstration plot for God's kingdom, then growing as disciples of Jesus Christ requires our working with multiple soil types through various stages of growth. Returning to the metaphor of a demonstration plot, we can identify four stages of discipleship: (1) preparing the soil; (2) planting the seed; (3) cultivating and weeding; and

(4) harvesting. These can be subdivided into the following phases: the cautious seeker, the curious inquirer, the committed member, the called disciple, the tested disciple, the transformed disciple, and the entrusted disciple (see fig. 3.1).

Preparing the Soil

Each spring, I till my garden long before I plant the first seeds. Heavy rains, together with winter's freezing and thawing, have compacted the soil. It is as hard as concrete. Tilling breaks up the hard soil and creates a soft bed for seeds. It loosens the soil so it can absorb water and the sun's warmth. The first stage of discipleship likewise involves preparing our lives so they are receptive to God's spirit. Preparing the soil includes two phases of discipleship development: cautious seekers and curious inquirers.

Cautious Seekers. Cautious seekers are a diverse group, falling into at least three categories. Cautious seekers may have a sense

FIGURE 3.1
Stages and Phases of Discipleship

Stage	Phase
A. Preparing the soil	1. The cautious seeker
	2. The curious inquirer
B. Planting the seed	3. The committed member
	4. The called disciple
C. Cultivating and weeding	5. The tested disciple
	6. The transformed disciple
D. Harvesting	7. The entrusted disciple

that something is missing from their lives. They have questions about the meaning of life or about God, but they are often reluctant to seek answers from Christian congregations. Other seekers have a history of hurt with the church. They may have grown up in a church that was oppressive, conflicted, or judgmental. Consequently, they feel wounded by Christian congregations and do not want to be hurt again. Finally, some cautious seekers are church members who have experienced burnout because they became over-involved. Overwhelmed by too much doing and too little meaning, they dropped out and never came back.

Curious Inquirers. Some cautious seekers become curious inquirers. Curious inquirers have taken the risk of attending Sunday worship or another church activity. Curious inquirers often come for a brief period and then disappear for months, only to reappear unexpectedly. They are testing the waters, asking, "What am I going to do about this?" They can take a long time to answer this question. Usually they are asking if this particular congregation will help them satisfy a hunger or yearning they feel within themselves. Although they cannot clearly name this yearning, it is a hunger for God.

Preparing for Cautious Seekers. Getting ready to plant my seeds takes more time than anything else I do in the garden. I have to clean away winter's debris, till the soil, lay out the rows, buy seeds, and assemble my tools. In the same way, preparing the soil for cautious seekers and curious inquirers requires more time than any other stage of discipleship development. Preparing the soil cannot be rushed. God's grace has its own schedule, which usually does not match our human timetable. Responding to seekers is not a one-time event. It is a long-term process.

The first point of contact for most cautious seekers is usually a coworker, neighbor, or family member. Being a person of spiritual influence is therefore every disciple's responsibility. A seeker's future openness to God may depend on one disciple's witness. More often, it requires many witnesses over a long period of time. Peter advises us to "always be ready to make your defense to anyone who demands from you an accounting for the hope that is in you; yet do it with gentleness and reverence" (1 Pet. 3:15-16).

Many church members have forgotten the difference Jesus Christ has made in their own lives. They therefore find it difficult to give an account of the hope that is within them. Each congregation needs to consider ways it can create opportunities to help people recall their own experiences of transformation and be able to speak about them in simple, nonthreatening ways to cautious seekers.

I know of a congregation that includes a component on faith sharing in its leadership training. The basic format asks participants to share their answers to three questions:

1. What was your life like prior to becoming a follower of Jesus Christ? If you cannot remember a time apart from the love of God, describe a period in your life when you drifted away from God temporarily.
2. What is one event or experience that helped you grow in your relationship to God in Christ, particularly that brought you to follow Jesus Christ or brought you back after a time of drifting?
3. Where is one place in your life that God is working right now? What are the signs of transformation you see in your life?

Over time, a critical mass of participants has learned to testify to the hope within them. They are creating a congregational culture where disciples of Jesus Christ can share their testimonies with grace and sensitivity.

While scripture tells us that disciples are witnesses, it does not demand that we engage in "witnessing." I have been accosted by strangers who handed me a tract, asked me about the state of my soul, or questioned the authenticity of my baptism. A friend once described this approach as "dive-bomb witnessing." Eager evangelists swoop down on unsuspecting strangers and leave them feeling manipulated and overpowered. Human beings are not "cold contacts" but rather children of God with wounds and hopes, fears and questions. They need a witness who stands *with* them, not someone witnessing *at* them. To be a witness is less about what we say than who we are.

By listening deeply to seekers, the disciple as a witness helps seekers discern where God is already active in their lives. Such testimony demands an awareness of one's own inner journey as well as a sensitivity to the experiences of others. When we are witnesses, we share our faith in a natural rather than a forced way. Awareness of the Spirit's movement in someone's life cannot be forced or imposed because freedom itself is an essential characteristic of Jesus' followers. If we are genuinely interested in people and ask meaningful questions about their lives, we prepare the soil for their discerning of the God who is already with them.

Congregations should also think carefully about how they create opportunities for cautious seekers to experience Christian community. Our congregation sponsors several events to which we make a special effort to invite inquirers or seekers. We have game nights where everyone brings a board game to play. On the Sunday nearest Saint Francis's feast day, we host a pet blessing that is followed by light refreshments or a program on pet care. We also partner with organizations in the community that share some but not all of our values. By partnering with groups that address important community issues, disciples of Jesus Christ work alongside people who otherwise might never come to know them. In these interactions, stereotypes held by cautious seekers can be corrected and their histories of hurt healed.

Preparing for Curious Inquirers. Curious inquirers are cautious seekers who have risked entering our doors for worship or another church activity. Like many churches, our congregation keeps careful attendance records. We are not a megachurch. On a typical Sunday we have 100 to 120 people in worship. We can easily identify visitors. We take the usual recommended steps to encourage their return. A few come back the following Sunday, telling us we are exactly the church they have been looking for. Some never return because we are clearly not for them. We pay special attention, however, to a third group. These are people who may not return for several months. Then they will attend a few Sundays in a row only to disappear again. Sometimes this haphazard attendance will continue for a year or more. These irregular visitors are curious inquirers.

How do we prepare the soil for curious inquirers? Churches need to stay in touch and communicate with curious inquirers on an intentional, ongoing basis. Too often we assume that if someone does not come back, they are not interested. Curious inquirers are not disinterested, however. They just take a long time to test the waters. It is precisely during this period of testing that they need to hear from us. Staying in touch encourages curious inquirers to realize we are genuinely interested in them and do not see them only as "prospects for membership." Our congregation assumes that sporadic visitors are curious seekers, and we stay in touch with them unless they deliberately contact us and say they are not interested.

The congregation in which I worship adds the names of these inquirers to a database so they receive a weekly e-mail message. These messages are meant to inspire, to provoke thought, and to help people make meaningful connections of scripture to everyday experiences. Where possible, we subdivide inquirers into interest groups. If we know they have children of a certain age, they receive additional e-mails about events for children and youth. Other inquirers receive targeted e-mails about study groups or mission trips. One congregation has made a special effort to invite inquirers to participate in its mission trips. Leaders see these trips as a way to move inquirers to a point of commitment. Once they spend a week with others on a mission trip, they usually find themselves ready for a new level of commitment.

It is often easier for a curious inquirer to enter the church through some event other than Sunday worship. Mission trips, game nights, potluck dinners, and other activities can serve as portals through which a cautious seeker may enter and gradually become a curious inquirer. Many congregations use small-group strategies and cell-church models to move inquirers toward the next steps in discipleship. Congregations can also explore a multitude of informal, relational strategies that are adaptable to their specific context.

All four Gospels describe Jesus as surrounded by followers who fell into several different circles of commitment. He had an inner circle of disciples, a larger circle of followers, and a still larger "crowd" that accompanied him in his travels. Some people who follow Jesus are always going to be part of the curious but cautious crowd around him. Others will become his supporters and followers. Still others become deeply committed as disciples. All three groups are pilgrims seeking God's kingdom. All deserve nurture and prayer as well as opportunities for growth and challenges appropriate to their particular stage along the way. The journey of faith occurs over a long period of time. People sometimes make small, incremental steps that lead to bigger moments of commitment. We cannot make this process fit our desired time lines. It is the work of the Spirit. It is not ours to manage and control, but it is ours to support and empower. Sometimes our strongest witness to God's reign is the authenticity of our care for those who are curious yet cautious about following Jesus.

Each congregation needs to assess what types of cautious seekers and curious inquirers are located in its community. If our vision of discipleship begins and ends only with active church members, we easily overlook the larger circles of those who are seeking Jesus. We miss opportunities to welcome the crowd around Jesus into more intimate circles of discipleship with him. Information about cautious seekers and curious inquirers permits congregational leaders to design locally effective strategies for these groups. The key issue for leaders and congregations is to remember that they minister *with and among* the curious and the cautious, not *to* them.

Planting the Seed

Once the soil is tilled, my home garden is ready for planting. Not every seed is the same, however. I plant peas as early as possible in cool soil. Cucumber seeds need warm soil, so I plant them much later. Depending on the seeds, different depths and spacing of rows are required. In the same way, transforming inquirers into disciples requires attention to unique differences. The stage of planting the seed includes two phases: the committed member and the called disciple.

Committed Members. Committed members fit their church commitments into their existing schedules. They do not rearrange their schedules to make congregational involvement a priority. Their participation is typically based on a commitment to a particular person or group in the congregation. Committed members fill the membership rolls of many congregations.

Called Disciples. Called disciples are people who feel called to a more intentional following of Jesus. They have experienced God's love and acceptance. This experience of justifying grace produces a transformation in their lives. This is the moment when people actually begin their journey as disciples. We have been calling them seekers, inquirers, or members up to this point. Now we can call them disciples. Called disciples seek opportunities to learn more about the Bible and the Christian tradition. They learn about spiritual disciplines. They seek out groups where they can serve. Called disciples no longer see church involvement as what they do when they have no other conflicting commitments. They adjust their schedules to make Christ their first priority.

From Curiosity to Call. How can congregations create opportunities for spiritual pilgrims to experience God's grace, love, and acceptance? Many people find love and acceptance in small groups, but small groups are not the only places where people have these experiences. Furthermore, many committed members do not participate in small groups. If the congregation's focus is on small groups as the only vehicle for transformative experiences, what about all those who opt out of small groups?

Other options are possible. Worship is an obvious leverage point for experiences of grace and inclusion. In one congregation, planners carefully design worship and prayer experiences during the Lenten and Easter seasons to create opportunities for people to experience grace, acceptance, and love. Retreat and camping opportunities are other frequently overlooked possibilities for transformative experiences. We recognize the importance of camping and retreat experiences for children and youth. Why do we assume they do not offer the same opportunities for adults? Mission trips can encourage experiences that move people to called discipleship.

Church leaders would also do well to examine their organizational and administrative life for how it provides opportunities to experience acceptance and grace. Acceptance becomes a very practical matter in a church committee: Does my voice matter? Are my suggestions valued or derided? Am I seen for who I am or do I have to hide part of myself? How do people respond when someone's project fails or when someone makes a mistake? Are they met with grace and understanding or accusation and blame? Church boards, councils, and committees demonstrate the plausibility of God's reign when their common life is marked by values of grace and inclusion, acceptance and new beginnings.

None of this happens overnight. The worst solution is to preach a sermon series on the stages of discipleship and think this one-time, one-way communication will shift the congregation's culture. Creating a congregational culture that nurtures discipleship is a long-term process.

From Membership to Discipleship. Despite what membership vows say, unspoken congregational norms typically set expectations for discipleship no higher than the level of committed membership. As long as the congregation's spiritual thermostat is set at this level, few people will rise to the level of called discipleship.

How, then, do church leaders raise the threshold of expectations for discipleship? New member orientation represents one high-leverage opportunity for changing congregational norms over time. When people enter an organization, they are open to learning its expected norms. Changing people's expectations as they enter the congregation can gradually create a critical mass of people who have a new, higher threshold for discipleship.

Some congregational leaders do not call these groups "new membership classes" or "membership orientation classes" because they want to reach a broad range of participants and not just those seeking membership. Hence, they adopt titles that appeal to everyone, from seekers and inquirers to members and disciples. One congregation retitled its newcomer orientation class "Compass-Points" because its leaders wanted to eliminate the perception that this group was only for newcomers. It was for anyone wanting an "orientation" to the congregation and its ministries.

This congregation's class includes a module on the stages of discipleship. As participants discuss this module, they realize church membership is not a static category but rather an ongoing pilgrimage. A second module introduces the congregation's various ministries, classes, and groups. It challenges participants to identify how each setting contributes to their own growth as disciples of Jesus Christ. Without creating a rigid system of basic and elective courses, leaders gently guide participants toward settings that facilitate their growth as disciples. Another module invites participants to develop a personal development plan for discipleship.

Congregations can also incorporate a multistage discipleship model into the annual stewardship campaign. Church members and participants are challenged to be responsible stewards of their own spiritual journeys. In other congregations, leaders will introduce a stage model of discipleship development for officer orientation and committee training. Over time, an awareness of discipleship as an ongoing process rather than a static goal permeates the whole congregation's culture. The ultimate goal is to reset people's expectations so they see discipleship as a journey of transformation and growth rather than as a steady state to be attained.

Worship planners also have opportunities to readjust low expectations for discipleship. One critical step entails careful planning of the reception of new members and baptisms. These two events are threshold moments when people enter the congregation. As such, they are important norming moments. Worship both expresses and forms a congregation's faith. Looking at the words and actions of baptism and reception of new members thus constitutes another high-leverage intervention.

Finally, church leaders sometimes inadvertently convey the idea that more participation equals more discipleship (i.e., the more church activities you attend, the more you grow as a disciple). But this is not necessarily true. When it comes to growing as a disciple, the key variable is not more participation but the kind of participation. Is it participation that moves someone's journey forward? Or does it unconsciously keep people in their comfort zones so they avoid experiences that foster growing discipleship? When leaders inadvertently equate more participation with more discipleship, they create the conditions for burnout: people do more and more but find less and less meaning or joy in their involvement.

Equating more participation with more discipleship can also encourage complacency. So long as people are attending more activities and going to worship more often, they can conclude that they are growing. The difference between called discipleship and committed membership, however, is one of quality, not just quantity. What matters are experiences of acceptance and love, not more activities on one's calendar.

Cultivating and Weeding

Eventually, my seeds grow into plants. But I am always amazed at how much more quickly weeds sprout than plants in my garden. Unless I regularly cultivate and weed, these unwanted guests soon choke out my plants. In the same way, disciples inevitably face weeds and thorns that threaten to choke off their progress as followers of Jesus Christ. The third stage of discipleship involves cultivating and weeding and has two phases: the tested disciple and the transformed disciple.

Tested Disciples. Eventually, every disciple experiences a crisis of faith. Personal crises turn their worlds upside down and cause them to question whether God really loves them. Someone in the church might betray them or judge them harshly, especially when they have worked hard on a special project or ministry. A destructive conflict might lead them to question the church's authenticity. An important project might fail to bear fruit, resulting in a sense of failure or even shame. In some cases, no specific event triggers a crisis of faith. People simply find less meaning and joy in their discipleship.

All these experiences are what the medieval Spanish mystic Saint John of the Cross called "the dark night of the soul." According to John of the Cross, we are mostly in love with experiences of praying, serving, or learning during the early stages of our spiritual pilgrimage. These experiences matter more to us than our love of God itself. The dark night withdraws the joy of these secondary loves so we can discover the love of God for its own sake. When we hit the wall and experience the dark night of the soul, we begin to ask questions: Why doesn't my faith work any longer? Why has the joy in my discipleship left me?

There is no easy way through this stage. The dark night of the soul is not a one-time experience. It can recur. It might last a short time or linger for long periods of dryness and emptiness.

The main task when we experience a dark night of the soul is to stay with our pain and confusion rather than run from it or deny it. We have to refocus our energy from the outward journey to the inward one. Spiritual disciplines and practices become the map and compass for this inward pilgrimage. These disciplines may be the same ones we were practicing before a crisis of faith. Now, however, we practice them for the sake of our relationship with God, not for the good feelings engendered when we pray, testify, or serve others.

Transformed Disciples. The onset of this stage is marked by a growing sense of feeling at home with ourselves and God once again. We accept that the questions troubling us during our dark nights may not have answers. So we are more able to live with the questions. We arrive at a point where we love the questions themselves, although we may still sometimes feel spiritually and emotionally empty.

Then, one day, we return to many of the practices and ministries we were doing before. Only now we do them with a different spirit. We have a greater freedom in our discipleship. We are less attached to the results of our ministries. We may be less driven to be the "best disciple possible." We minister and witness from a more grounded center. We encounter the Bible and our devotional reading with new insights. We find ourselves making new connections between our lives and God's Word.

Supporting the Tested and Transformed Disciple. When called disciples enter a dark night of the soul, their greatest need is for spiritual mentors and spiritual friends to walk the path with them. Unfortunately, the church often shoots its own wounded. Leaders blame these disciples for a "lack of faith" and accuse them of "backsliding." These responses can be hurtful and sometimes turn a called disciple into an embittered, cautious seeker.

Tested disciples need the support of others who have already walked this part of the journey. Disciples who have passed through a dark night of the soul and come out on the other side can provide them with spiritual direction and guidance. Accountable discipleship groups are a critical resource for both tested and transformed disciples. In these small-group settings, they can deal honestly with their feelings and fears. Group members have an opportunity to provide support and accountability for the practice of spiritual disciplines that will ultimately pull them through this phase of their own journeys.

An understanding of the spiritual and theological resources of the Christian tradition is also invaluable to disciples experiencing the dark night of the soul. The wisdom of Saint John of the Cross, Georgia Harkness, and other devotional writers can serve as a source of encouragement and insight. Helping disciples grow in Christ means guiding them along the paths others have traveled before.

Sabbath keeping occupies an especially important role in this phase of discipleship development. In the work of creation, God's energy was pushed to the limit. On the seventh day, God rested for renewal. As called disciples, it is possible for our ministries to deplete our spiritual and physical energy. All disciples—and especially those experiencing a period of spiritual emptiness—need sabbath time. Sabbath helps us purge the drivenness related to *doing* from our discipleship. One important way church leaders can support disciples during their dark nights of the soul is to give them permission for sabbath. Leaders can protect them from the demands of others. Patience, pastoral care, and good spiritual guidance help tested disciples make sense of their paths through the darkness. When they come out of this experience, they are ready for a new level of participation in God's mission to heal a broken world.

Harvesting

The fourth and final stage of discipleship is harvesting. Entrusted disciples have passed through the dark night of the soul. This experience has purged from their discipleship much of their own self-interest. They no longer serve or pray or lead for the good feelings these activities may generate. Freed from themselves, they are free to give themselves for others and to God. Entrusted disciples of Jesus Christ frequently have insights that make them excellent coaches or mentors.

Entrusted disciples are growing disciples, but they are also disciples who help others grow. Congregational leaders need to look continually for opportunities to equip entrusted leaders with the skills to lead and facilitate learning, doing, and decision-making groups in the congregation. Entrusted disciples are seasoned disciples who have a larger picture of what it means to follow Jesus. They have the perspective and experience to serve as spiritual directors and guides for others who are on the journey.

Stages of Discipleship and God's Grace

The four stages of discipleship are intertwined with the working of God's grace in our lives. John Wesley speaks of three types of grace: prevenient, justifying, and sanctifying grace.

Prevenient grace is the grace that goes before us. Through prevenient grace, God leads us, often without our conscious awareness, toward committing ourselves to God. Prevenient grace acts among cautious seekers, curious inquirers, and committed members, leading them to an encounter with justifying grace.

Justifying grace describes God's offer of forgiveness and new life, to which we respond in trust and gratitude. Through experiences of love and acceptance, we come to accept God's acceptance of us. Justifying grace breaks into our lives when we realize that we are not continuously on trial before a hostile judge. We are instead loved completely by the One who creates and sustains not just our own lives but life itself. We experience justifying grace in the love and acceptance that transform us from committed members to called disciples.

Sanctifying grace represents our ongoing growth as tested, transformed, and entrusted disciples. Empowered by the Holy Spirit, we become increasingly free to give ourselves to others in the same way that Jesus poured himself out in a life of self-giving love. Freed from justifying ourselves, we are free for God and others. Marks of ongoing sanctification include maturing as hearers of God's Word, growth in prayer, and freedom to serve the needs of others.

Figure 3.2 describes the relationship between God's grace and the various stages and phases of discipleship.

CREATING SYSTEMS THAT HELP PEOPLE GROW AS DISCIPLES OF JESUS CHRIST

An overall picture of discipleship development provides congregational leaders with a framework for approaching their work more intentionally. Too often our approaches to forming disciples of Jesus Christ are either magical or managerial.

Some congregations have a haphazard approach to discipleship development. Cultural assumptions about individualism often cause church leaders to assume that each individual has the sole responsibility for his or her development as a disciple. Leaders offer a wide spectrum of activities and classes, mostly based on people's expressed interests. They then leave it up to the individual to decide which settings foster her or his growth. People make these choices based on what sounds interesting rather than what may stretch them beyond their comfort zone and lead them to the next stage of discipleship. Leaders thus assume that people will somehow grow magically without much planning, direction, or intentionality.

FIGURE 3.2
God's Grace and the Stages of Discipleship

PREPARING THE SOIL		PLANTING THE SEED	
Prevenient Grace		Justifying Grace	
Cautious	Curious	Committed	Called
Cynical about organized religion	Takes risk of showing up	Participation becomes regular	Has deeper experience of Christ's love and acceptance
History of hurt by church, family	Willing to engage in some group settings, worship or another point of entry	Extends relationships beyond original acquaintances or group	Actively seeks ways to grow in love of God and neighbor (disciplines, bible study, service, and outreach)
Life full, busy		May volunteer to participate in service or outreach	
Searching for answer to some question	May participate then disappear for weeks or months only to reappear	Explores Bible and how to learn or study it	Makes participation in the community a priority rather than one commitment among many
Sense that there must be more to life		May inquire about spiritual disciplines	May be able to talk about experiences and reflect on them
		Commitment is more to group, friends, or person than to Christ	Exhibits growing willingness to share Christ's love with others through generosity, hospitality, and service

WEEDING AND CULTIVATING	HARVESTING
Sanctifying Grace	

Tested	Transformed	Entrusted
"Hits the wall"	Deepens inward journey	Freedom in Christ from the self so has expanded freedom to be for and with others
Personal crisis turns world upside down	Reflects on experience in a new way, making new connections to Bible and Christian theological tradition	
Loss of meaning and joy in relationship with Christ		Less compulsion and personal need in ministries in which involved
Experiences a sense of failure in what he or she has been trying to do for God	Often needs a guide or mentor to help walk through "dark night of soul"	Greater openness to other perspectives and experiences in his or her hospitality
Feels ministry is misunderstood, criticized, rejected by congregation	Experiences a deeper sense of freedom in relationship to Christ	Generous in use of time, abilities, and money in service of Christ's mission in the world
Has shattering experience of betrayal, criticism, or conflict in congregation	May continue doing much of what was doing before during this period but experiences little meaning in it	Able to reflect on experiences theologically and to help others think about their own experiences
		Active leadership in outreach, service, and ministry
		Coach and mentor others in their discipleship

Other congregational leaders adopt a managerial approach. They implement rigid structures and pathways for discipleship development. They have fixed ideas about how people grow. As a result, they attempt to manage the work of the Spirit. Adult groups and classes are divided into basic and elective courses. Leaders expect people to complete basic courses before they can advance into elective courses. Just as children's Sunday schools have often organized themselves around curricular models of public education, these managerial models frequently borrow from higher education's framework of introductory and advanced courses, prerequisites, and fixed curricular sequences.

We need a perspective that moves beyond both magical and managerial approaches to discipleship development. Disciples do not just mysteriously grow. Congregational leaders must set expectations for growth and provide guidance about how to grow and offer specific, structured opportunities for growth. On the other hand, the Spirit's work cannot be managed in the same structured, linear, sequential way used by elementary schools to teach children to read or do long division. There must be enough structure to guide people toward appropriate options but not so much structure that it becomes the main focus of attention.

A more flexible approach begins by asking questions like these:

1. How do we prepare and encourage committed members and disciples to witness to cautious seekers? Does our congregation have formal training to help people testify and witness to their faith? Are there ways we informally build these capacities as people engage in other ministries and activities?

2. How can we provide opportunities for cautious seekers to interact with our congregation and help them move beyond stereotypes they may have or heal hurts they have previously experienced?

3. What are some ways we can intentionally stay in touch with curious inquirers? Do we identify them and track them over time?

4. Do we see ourselves as ministering *with* and *among* the cautious or curious? Or do we see ourselves as only ministering *to* them?

5. How do we encourage curious inquirers to move toward committed membership? If the initial commitment is to a particular individual or group, how can we foster a deeper commitment to Jesus Christ through relationships and not merely programs?

6. Do our thresholds of expectation encourage people to believe committed membership is the last and final stage of discipleship? If so, what are the leverage points for shifting expectations of growth beyond committed membership?

7. Do we actually believe God changes lives? How do we create both formal and informal opportunities for people to experience the transforming power of God's love and acceptance?

8. Do we acknowledge the dark night of the soul in ways that affirm it as an inevitable part of the discipleship journey? Do we help people navigate this stage of discipleship or do we blame them when they express a loss of spiritual meaning?

9. What formal and informal support do we provide for tested and transformed disciples? Are there accountability groups or spiritual directors for them?

10. Do we fully employ the gifts of entrusted disciples? How do we encourage them to continue growing?

11. Do we plan settings for growth at every stage of discipleship development? Or is it acceptable to leave some phases unserved? Just because a congregation lacks people living through a particular phase of discipleship, does this absence eliminate the responsibility to plan intentional growth opportunities for this stage? If we do not plan for a particular phase, are we saying that people in this phase are not welcome in our congregation?

12. What role do we envision for small groups as vehicles for discipleship development? Are small groups the only strategy we pursue or are they part of a larger repertoire of options?

13. Do we envision a small-group ministry that consists mostly of long-term groups or short-term groups? Does it matter? Are short-term or long-term groups more appropriate for some stages of discipleship formation in our congregation? If so, how do we connect people with a group right for them?

14. What intentional efforts do we make to provide spiritual mentors, coaches, or guides? How are these mentors and directors trained and supported? How do mentors and spiritual guides relate to our small-group ministries?

15. How do we ensure that the whole life of the congregation, particularly its boards, councils, and committees, fosters discipleship development? Do we instead assume that all responsibility for discipleship development belongs to Christian education committees or small-group ministries?

An approach to discipleship development that is neither magical nor managerial begins with these questions. It seeks to move people from cautious seekers to entrusted disciples not so much through classes and small groups—as important as these are to developing disciples of Jesus Christ—but rather by apprenticing them into a community of people who together practice being disciples of Jesus Christ.

For Further Reflection

1. Draw a personal time line of your growth as a disciple of Jesus Christ.

   - List major markers along your journey.
   - What are the events or people that sparked a significant change in your discipleship?
   - What are the chapters into which you can divide your journey? If you could give each chapter a title, what would it be?
   - How do the chapters of your spiritual journey seem similar or different from those outlined in this chapter? Do you see them as discrete stages unfolding in a linear way, or do you see yourself as cycling through one or more of these stages repeatedly in your life?

2. Complete the chart on the next page (fig. 3.3).
   Once you have completed the chart, discuss these questions:

   - Not all ministries occur on a weekly or even a monthly basis. Are there special events throughout the year like mission trips, retreats, a church bazaar, or an annual homecoming dinner that could play a role in forming disciples? What role do these events play and whom do they serve? How could their contribution to disciple-making be enhanced?
   - Some opportunities for growth in discipleship are sponsored by agencies outside the congregation. For example, camping and conferencing events are frequently managed by districts, annual conferences, or other formal or informal

FIGURE 3.3

Events, ministries, groups in our congregation*	What stage of discipleship is this group, event, or ministry primarily intended to serve?†	What stage of discipleship is this activity promoted for in announcements, from the pulpit, in the newsletter, or website?	What stage of discipleship are the majority of those who participate in this ministry, activity, or group?	Does this ministry, group, or event intentionally help participants know what to do next if they are interested in growing as a disciple?

*If you are from a large congregation, you may want to break down this exercise into specific congregational subunits (education, mission, worship, and other ministry areas) to make it more manageable.

†The word *primarily* is emphasized because a single activity or group may serve more than one stage of adult faith formation. Try to avoid the temptation to list every group as serving all stages. Think critically about the primary audience and the primary goal you have for this group or activity.

associations of churches. What are these events and activities? What role do they play in the adult faith formation of your congregation?

- Is your approach to making disciples of Jesus Christ magical, managerial, or flexibly intentional? What evidence would you give to support your conclusion?

- What assumptions is your congregation making about how people grow as disciples based on the kinds of activities and ministries you sponsor?

- In what stage (or stages) of discipleship do most of your activities assume their audience to be?

- What stage (or stages) of discipleship do most of your activities and events overlook or leave underserved? If there are gaps, what might you do to close or bridge them?

- What is one action your congregation can take that would make a big difference for followers of Jesus Christ who want to grow as disciples?

- Are there scheduled activities within your congregation that do not contribute to making disciples? If these activities cannot be adapted to disciple-making, should you continue to invest in them?

CHAPTER FOUR

APPRENTICED AS MEMBERS
OF A DISCIPLING COMMUNITY

Discipleship is a journey. As followers of Jesus Christ, we progress through multiple stages that unfold across our lifetimes. We experience periods of growth and consolidation. We encounter detours and dead ends. Our pilgrimages take us through dark valleys, across tedious plateaus, and along refreshing streams. What sustains us on these pilgrimages? What energizes our growth? What reorients us when we have lost our way? Six discipleship practices, discussed in chapter 2 and summarized below, anchor and center us as we make this journey. They play a critical role in our pilgrimages of growing in the love, knowledge, and service of God and neighbor. While discipleship evolves through different stages and phases, these practices remain constant.

DISCIPLESHIP PRACTICES: BREAD
FOR THE JOURNEY

Six fundamental discipleship practices characterize all stages of discipleship: growing in biblical literacy, practicing spiritual disciplines, cultivating hospitality and generosity, engaging in service and outreach, discerning our experience of God, and testifying to God's presence in our lives.

We do not outgrow these practices. Nor are some practices reserved only for advanced disciples. These practices are integral to all stages of discipleship. We do, however, build and broaden them as we grow. They take on greater depth. We practice them in more intuitive and holistic ways. Our performance becomes more complex as we recognize how these practices mutually enhance and support one another.

Just as God gave bread to the people of Israel when they wandered hungry in the wilderness, God gives us these practices as bread for the journey. They sustain and support us along the way. They guide us to experiences of God's love and acceptance. They build spiritual reserves that uphold us when we are tested and transformed. They nourish us when we are depleted and discouraged. They center us as entrusted disciples. Discipleship practices nurture our growth. These practices transform us so we grow as coparticipants with God in transforming the world.

Discipleship Practices Build and Broaden

How can church leaders encourage followers of Jesus Christ to build and broaden their performance of these practices? Researchers have studied how people acquire knowledge, attitudes, skills, and habits. Their insights help us understand how followers of Jesus Christ learn discipleship practices. Hubert L. Dreyfus and Stuart E. Dreyfus (1986, 16–35) have developed a widely accepted five-stage typology for how practicing professionals grow: novices, advanced beginners, competent practitioners, proficient practitioners, and expert practitioners.

According to their typology, novices learn objective facts and fixed rules that outside authorities have given to them. They gather information about a practice. As they gain experience, however, their perceptions and skills are formed by what they are doing. Finally, experts no longer "have" a practice. They "are" their practice. As practitioners grow, they evolve through stages of gathering information about a practice, being formed through experience, and, finally, personally transformed by it.

Think for a moment about how you learned to drive a car. As a beginner, you learned objective facts about cars and driving. You then followed rigid rules about turn signals, speed limits, and coming to a complete stop. You had to think about each step individually when making a left-hand turn: pushing the turn signal, taking your foot off the gas and putting it on the brake, turning the steering wheel, checking your side and rearview mirrors, and watching for oncoming traffic. You thought about each step individually and performed each one consciously and sequentially. Eventually, you became an expert driver who combined all these individual steps into one flowing, coordinated action that you perform almost automatically. In fact, you may sometimes feel as if the car is driving itself because your performance of these tasks is so fluid and automatic. Learning to drive a car illustrates the three phases of learning a practice: information, formation, and transformation.

When we learn discipleship practices, our performance evolves through these same stages. We begin by gathering information about discipleship, the Bible, and spiritual disciplines. As we start to engage in these practices, they form our habits and values. Over time, a more significant, transformative shift occurs. Our discipleship begins to happen through us and we are carried along by it. Discipleship is not something we do. It is who we are.

We take for granted that people know how to pray. Christian prayer does not necessarily come naturally, however. We learn how to pray. At first, a parent or caregiver probably taught us to bow our heads, close our eyes, and hold our hands in a certain way. They helped us memorize a bedtime prayer or a grace before meals. We prayed according to the rules that we were taught, giving careful attention to our posture and words. One day we found that we no longer had to put so much effort into consciously thinking about this sequence of words and actions. Our praying arose from a different place within us. Our prayer lives were forming us into people of prayer. Finally, we discovered that our prayer lives had transformed who we were as persons.

Discipleship Practices and the Stages of Discipleship

A relationship exists between these stages of information, formation, and transformation and how we progress through the phases of discipleship. Consider how committed members view the annual stewardship campaign: Let's say that church leaders have given two members, whom we'll call Kenon and LaToya Wilson, specific rules about tithing. The Wilsons consult a tithing chart to determine the amount they should pledge. As far as they are concerned, they have done enough when they have given what the chart says to give. Called disciples, on the other hand, have moved beyond rigid, externally derived rules. They have their own internal rules of thumb for generosity. LaToya and Kenon eventually begin to see their generosity as set within the larger framework of what the congregation is doing and what ministries are important to them. In addition to their tithe, they may give to special offerings or other causes. Transformed and entrusted disciples ultimately do not conduct a cost-benefit analysis, asking what they will receive in return for what they give. Having been formed by their practice of generosity, Kenon and LaToya arrive at a place where their generous giving flows from an understanding of how generosity both fosters spiritual growth and is a response to God's own generosity. As entrusted disciples, their generosity contributes to their own ongoing personal transformation and to the transformation of the world.

FIGURE 4.1
Relationship of Discipleship Stages to Discipleship Practices

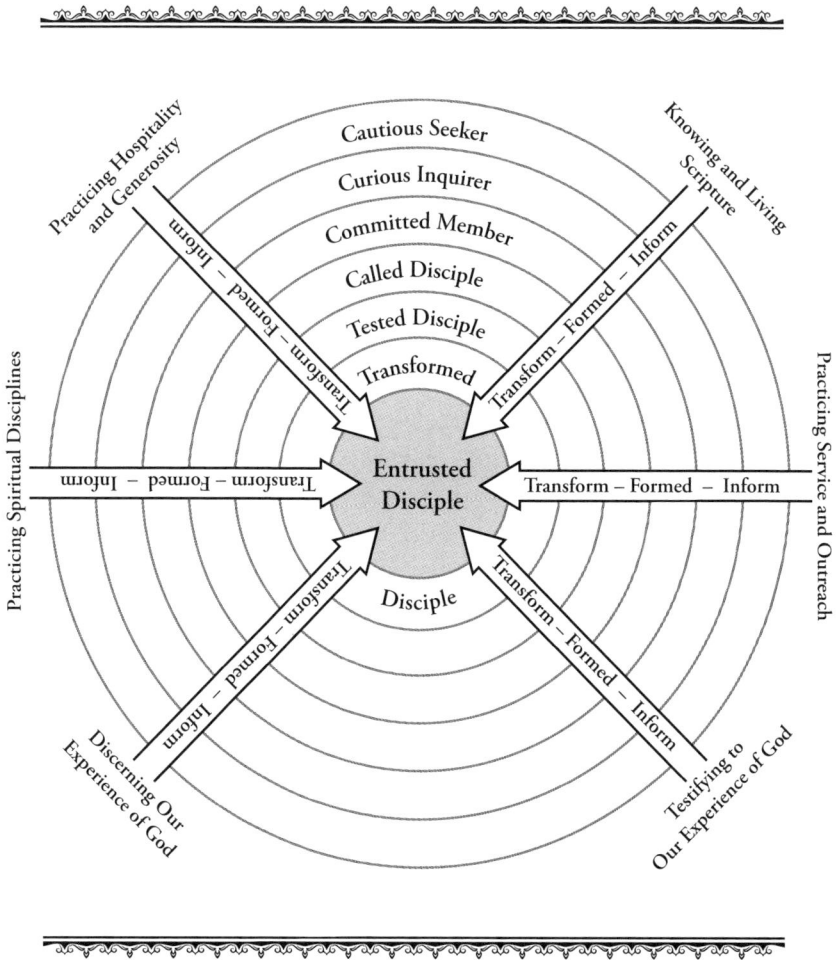

We can visualize the stages of discipleship as concentric circles orbiting around a center (see fig. 4.1).

The outermost circle represents cautious seekers whom prevenient grace has begun to pull into the orbit of God's love and acceptance. The circles nearer to the center represent the phases leading to entrusted discipleship. The vectors cutting across the seven circles are the six discipleship practices. These practices support a disciple's movement from the outer circle toward the center. At the outer edge of the circle, we are novices seeking information. As we progress toward the circle's hub, we move through a phase of practice that is more formative than informational. Finally, as we approach transformed and entrusted discipleship, our practices enter a transformative phase.

At the outer edge of the circle, we engage in practices self-consciously and often find ourselves thinking through each step of a practice. But the closer we come to entrusted discipleship, the more our discipleship practices become intuitive, complex, and deeply grounded within us. When we seek information about a practice, we tend to see each practice as something distinct and unrelated to the others. Then, as each spoke approaches the hub of entrusted discipleship, the closer each becomes to the others. In the same way, as we move from information to formation and then to transformation, we experience the six discipleship practices as drawing closer to one another. We see a web of mutually supportive disciplines rather than a smorgasbord of distinct activities.

As our discipleship practices become more formative and transformative, they move us toward transformed and entrusted discipleship. Conversely, the more our discipleship practices remain at the level of information seeking, the less energy they generate for our forward movement as disciples. Curious inquirers seek information. Entrusted disciples embrace ongoing transformation. Committed members want to know about their faith. Transformed disciples are what they know and believe. Their faith is a matter not of belief but of who they are, which expresses itself in what they do.

A ROAD MAP FOR DISCIPLESHIP PRACTICES AND STAGES

While discipleship practices and stages are mutually interactive, it is almost impossible to develop a specified scope and sequence for learning discipleship practices that undergirds growth as a disciple. People become disciples at different ages and times of their lives. They may participate sporadically, even as committed members. The twists and turns of their journeys may take them back to earlier stages of discipleship. There is no single discipleship practice that serves as a universal starting point. The process is nonlinear and fluid rather than fixed and predetermined. The model outlined here is only a starting point for one's own thinking and planning. In a different context, church leaders may wish to sort out and think through this process in a very different way.

Growing Through Knowing and Living Scripture

What does it look like for someone to grow as a disciple while simultaneously deepening her or his practice of knowing and living scripture? Carl went to Sunday school as a child but left after his confirmation. As a young adult, he became interested in history, including biblical history. He became increasingly curious about the Bible itself. He wanted more information about the biblical stories, about the people in the stories and the stories' meanings. He learned to find books, chapters, and verses. He learned the relationship between the Old and the New Testaments. Carl was in the Dreyfus model's novice or informational stage.

Carl gradually began to see the Bible as a whole document. He could describe how it came into its present form, how different writers contributed different perspectives, and how these perspectives relate to one another. He could group passages or images from different books into similar literary genres: the Law, the Prophets, the Wisdom writings, the Gospels, and the Epistles. He learned to identify different literary styles such as poetry, parables, and histories. Then came the ability to use a commentary, Bible atlas, and concordance. He has also become a committed member of his congregation's adult Bible class.

Carl's encounters with scripture soon became formative rather than informative. He began to read the Bible more regularly. He discovered themes that ran through the whole of scripture such as hospitality, grace, freedom, call, and covenant. These themes led him to other discipleship practices with which he was previously unfamiliar. Carl learned to describe how a particular story or parable relates to the Bible's larger themes and metaphors. He began to incorporate spiritual disciplines into his life such as *lectio divina*. His engagement with these disciplines formed him into a called disciple of Jesus Christ.

Finally, Carl's practice entered a transformative phase. Carl saw himself as a participant in God's unfolding biblical story, testifying to others and inviting them to see, receive, dwell within, and so participate in establishing God's reign on earth. He was able to witness to his faith, even when it was at odds with the culture around him. And he could critique society's practices in light of biblical themes and stories.

Growing Through the Practice of Spiritual Disciplines

Cautious seekers may be drawn to learning about spiritual practices. Chanelle started out browsing the "Body, Mind, Spirit" section in her local bookstore to find resources to help her cope with all the pressures of work and family. After reading several books, she wanted more information. Seeing a poster announcing classes on spiritual disciplines at a church near her home, she joined others in learning about the classic Christian disciplines: meditation, centering prayer, intercession, fasting, Christian conferencing, examination of conscience, and other inward, outward, and communal practices. Chanelle is a curious inquirer who is gathering objective information about spiritual disciplines.

Gradually, Chanelle found herself practicing these spiritual disciplines on a more consistent basis. She became a committed member of the church's spirituality group and occasionally attended worship. Over time, her interest in spiritual disciplines has moved from an informational to a formational stage. She has learned where to locate other resources for her spiritual growth such as seasonal devotional guides and prayer books. Practicing these spiritual disciplines formed Chanelle's attitudes, habits, and values over many months. She developed a familiarity with both contemporary and historical devotional writers such as the desert fathers and mothers, Saint Augustine, Saint Francis, Teresa of Ávila, Thomas Merton, and Henri Nouwen. She discovered the relationship of the Christian year and worship to her growth as a disciple. As her discipleship practices deepened and broadened, she had more powerful experiences of God's love and acceptance. She felt called as a disciple of Jesus Christ.

At one point, Chanelle experienced a time of spiritual emptiness. The emotional benefits of prayer and meditation dried up. She felt empty and emotionless. Chanelle learned new ways of discerning

God's presence within her experience. She gradually moved beyond this dark night of the soul, supported by a sensitive spiritual director who introduced her to several discipleship practices that had not previously been part of her repertoire. Chanelle had entered a more transformative phase. She was able to testify to others about her experience of God's presence. She became a spiritual friend and guide to others in the congregation. She was asked to lead and teach spirituality classes and found this a meaningful way to share her gifts. Spiritual disciplines were no longer something she did. They became an expression of who she was as a disciple of Jesus Christ.

Practicing Hospitality and Generosity

The trajectories of hospitality and generosity also move through these same three stages of information, formation, and transformation. This shift again roughly parallels the movement from cautious seeking to entrusted discipleship. Cautious seekers and curious inquirers may begin this journey simply by experiencing the hospitality and generosity of other Christians. This experience leads them to want to learn more. Gradually, they learn to identify biblical stories of hospitality and generosity.

Over time, their practice of hospitality and generosity becomes more formative. They start to extend hospitality and generosity to others or to share stories of when they experienced God's generosity. They notice situations that call for hospitality or generosity. These encounters lead cautious seekers and curious inquirers to experience God's love and acceptance anew, which culminates in a formative call to more intentional discipleship. As entrusted disciples, hospitality arises out of their awareness of God's hospitality and generosity toward all creation. They use their resources and gifts in transformative ways by supporting their congregation and serving the world.

Practicing Service and Outreach

Building and broadening the practice of service and outreach follows a similar path from novice engagement to seasoned practice. Marty had dropped out of church in her early twenties because she felt churches were self-absorbed and interested only in their own status and prestige. But she did not abandon the value of serving others, which her childhood church had inculcated in her. Through a friend, she became interested in a homeless shelter operated by some local congregations. As she participated regularly in this mission project, she wanted more information about other ways to serve as well as about the congregation and its commitments. Eventually, she became a committed member of the congregation's mission efforts. Marty gathered information about poverty, homelessness, and what the church could do about these issues.

As a committed member of the congregation, her practice of mission and outreach gradually became more formative. Working alongside others, listening to stories of the homeless, and opening herself to encounters with people different from herself, Marty came to experience a deeper sense of God's love and acceptance for all people, including herself. Marty's journey through committed membership and called discipleship was accompanied by a deepening awareness of how spiritual disciplines supported her journey and how the biblical tradition had much to say about poverty and wealth. She began to make connections between many different discipleship practices. She realized how spiritual gifts, spiritual disciplines, testimony, hospitality, generosity, and other practices were deeply intertwined with the practice of service and outreach.

Marty's commitment to mission led her to "hit the wall." During her dark night of the soul, Marty was fortunate to have wise spiritual guides who helped her understand the meaning of sabbath and introduced her to other discipleship practices that balanced her earlier overemphasis on service and outreach. She gradually developed a more balanced discipleship that was rooted in multiple disciplines and practices. As a tested, transformed, and entrusted disciple, Marty's discipleship practices were transformative. She actively looked for opportunities to serve others both locally and around the world. She was not content simply to meet the personal needs of others. She also perceived how individual needs are rooted in issues of public policy and systemic injustice. Marty realized how practices of service and outreach cannot be sustained without spiritual disciplines and biblical reflection. Service enriches our knowing and living of scripture. Service without hospitality can be cold and uncaring.

While Marty began her journey with a commitment to one discipleship practice (service and outreach), over time she added more discipleship practices to her repertoire. There was an interactive and mutually reinforcing relationship between Marty's growth through the stages of discipleship and her deeper engagement in multiple discipleship practices.

Discernment of and Witness to God's Presence in Our Lives

People who are curious about Christian faith usually seek information about its special words and terminology. They may also want to obtain information about the heritage of non-Christian traditions. As they advance, they begin to recognize how beliefs or theology shape their values and actions. The language of Christian faith gradually begins to form how they think and act.

The dark night of the soul becomes an occasion for growing disciples to examine their hidden assumptions. It serves as an opportunity to reflect on their inner experiences, which deepens their practice of discerning the experience of God in their lives—even in what feels like the absence of God. They have an opportunity to question their assumptions about God, Jesus, and the Bible. They entertain new, unexplored perspectives about God, themselves, and the world. This stage invites disciples to a new awareness of who they are as children of God. Their discernment gradually forms a new sense of self, which initiates a transformation in their being and doing.

Emerging from this phase as transformed and entrusted disciples, they are able to witness to their experiences in transformative ways. As seasoned practitioners, they draw upon the insights of other practices to enhance their testimonies, using the vocabulary of the church's theologians and devotional writers as well as the Bible to describe their experiences. Their practice of hospitality and generosity allows them to enter with sensitivity into the experiences of others who hold different perspectives or values. They use the fruit of these experiences to provide leadership in congregational and community settings where they witness to God's love and grace.

The Practice of Discipleship Formation

Church leaders grow in their practice of caring for a congregation's discipleship development system as they give attention to the interaction among discipleship stages and discipleship practices. Leaders may be tempted to rigidly apply this model of how discipleship stages and practices interact to foster Christian growth. Perhaps this is an inevitable part of their learning a new practice. As they listen to people's experiences and observe congregational systems, their own practice of discipleship development will undoubtedly evolve through these same stages of information, formation, and transformation. They will gradually develop a more fluid, flexible grasp of what patterns of stages and practices are possible in different circumstances.

It is important to remember that the flow of phases and practices of discipleship formation is neither linear nor sequential. The sequence of informing, forming, and transforming may take alternative forms. It could be reversed, moving from transformation to information. Gerry went through a personal crisis. His father died, and six months later he and his wife divorced. Struggling to adjust, Gerry changed many things for the better in his life. At this vulnerable time, he turned to the church as a resource for maintaining the new life he was building for himself. Gerry began with transformation (a significant change in his life) and moved to formation (resources to form his life in ways that sustained his newly discovered identity as a follower of Jesus Christ).

Billie Jean was formed into the practices of faith as a child but never fully understood them. As a college student, she sought out information to help her understand her earlier formation. New information then sparked significant transformation in her understanding and led to a deeper commitment to discipleship. Billie Jean began with neither information nor transformation. She entered the process at the point of formation and worked her way back to information and then leaped forward to transformation.

In working with Christians struggling with their call to follow Jesus, I sometimes ask them to draw a chart that plots their assessment of their discipleship practices. I ask them to place a dot on each line indicating where they see themselves, with the center being a number 1 and the outer edge being a number 10. I then have them connect the dots with a solid line. The result might look something like figure 4.2 on the next page.

FIGURE 4.2
Personal Inventory of Discipleship Practices and Stages

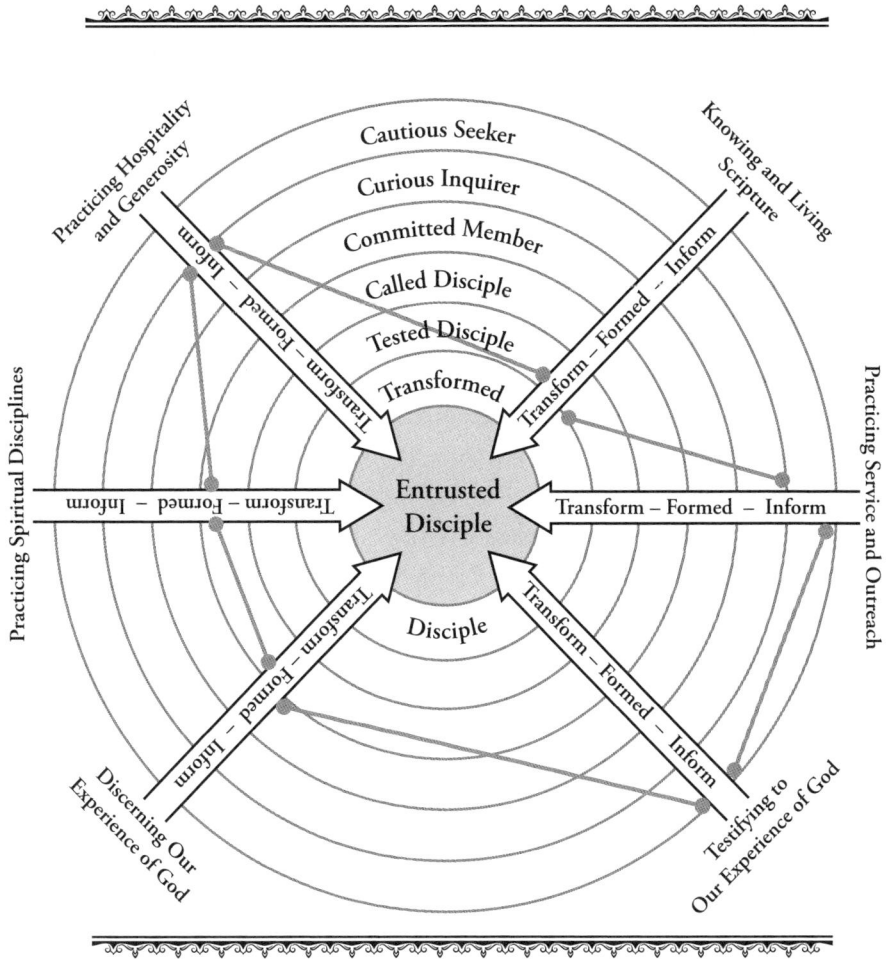

Cautious Seeker
Curious Inquirer
Committed Member
Called Disciple
Tested Disciple
Transformed

Entrusted
Disciple

Disciple

Practicing Hospitality and Generosity

Knowing and Living Scripture

Practicing Spiritual Disciplines

Practicing Service and Outreach

Discerning Our Experience of God

Testifying to Our Experience of God

Transform – Formed – Inform

Looking at this chart, we can see how an individual's discipleship practices can lack balance. One or two practices are pulling all the weight of his or her pilgrimage toward entrusted discipleship. A chart such as this can thus guide a conversation about what might be blocking this individual's growth as a disciple of Jesus Christ. I have often discovered that the practice most resisted is the one practice a disciple needs in order to grow. If people are going through dark-night experiences, preparing and discussing this chart can help them identify their points of vulnerability. It alerts them to early warning signals. It can be a source of insight and encouragement when they feel they have lost their way.

The concentric circles on this chart resemble the labyrinth's circuits. As with the labyrinth, we move along these discipleship pathways not alone but as part of a covenant community committed to the same path and practices. Completing the pathways individually could mislead us into thinking we take this journey alone. Others are always walking these paths with us. We never remain faithful to these discipleship practices alone. We are always practicing them together as the church. We may think we are moving forward under our own strength, but in reality, we are being carried forward by a whole community's faithful practice of discipleship.

Learning to Be a Member of a Discipling Community

An anthropologist named Julian E. Orr (1996) studied how photocopier service technicians learned and worked together. Orr's repair technicians faced a major challenge as novices. The company's repair manuals did not describe the problems technicians actually encountered. Breakdowns almost never matched the descriptions found in the manuals. Technicians consequently did not learn how to repair the machines from classes and books. What Orr discovered also serves to help us better understand how disciples grow.

The technicians instead became competent practitioners as they apprenticed themselves, if unofficially, to experienced technicians. Novices talked to more experienced workers about their service calls over coffee or at lunch. Seasoned employees told stories about difficult repairs. The novice technicians listened and learned. Faced with a challenging repair, they would call an expert technician for advice or watch one at work. The more seasoned technicians also benefited from these apprenticeships, helping the seasoned technicians stay fresh and keep growing.

According to Orr, the critical factor that defines a service technician is learning to be a member of a community of technicians that constantly improves its repair practices. In the same way, the critical factor is not just learning discipleship practices. It is learning to become a member of a community committed to these practices. We tend to think individualistically. Discipleship practices are not something I do alone and then contribute as a disciple to a community called church. I learn the practices of discipleship when I am apprenticed into a discipling community. "Community" is not another discipline I practice alongside all the others. It is the context in which I learn to be a disciple. We build and broaden our discipleship practices by learning to be members of a covenant community whose common life constantly rehearses the practices that embody the love, knowledge, and service of God and neighbor. Jesus, as I said earlier, never had just one disciple. From the very beginning, he has called people into a community gathered around him that shares in his mission.

Discipleship is not a competency that I individually acquire and personally possess. I can go to class after class and small group after small group. I can attend worship for years and listen to hundreds of sermons. But all these activities do not make me a disciple. I learn to be a disciple of Jesus Christ by apprenticing myself to him within a covenant community of people who are also committed to growing as disciples and who together perform the practices that embody God's mission to heal a broken world.

Apprentices in a Community of Shared Practice

"Apprentice" is a better translation for the New Testament Greek word for "disciple" than the more common translation of "learner." Our individualistic assumptions too easily distort "learning" into something we do privately and possess individually. Apprenticeship expresses the essence of what it means to be a member of a community of shared practice. Working alongside mentors and colleagues, apprentices are not just learning a particular skill. They are learning to become members of a community of shared practice.

Learning is built from the materials at hand and in relation to the people and resources available. People do not start with a set of blueprints, buy all the materials for discipleship, and then learn to be disciples. Their learning is episodic, based on observing and apprenticing themselves to others. Learning emerges from our conversations, personal sharing, and from the numerous situations in which we find ourselves. Situations at hand provide the primary material with which to work.

We live within the Mississippi flyway. Every spring and autumn thousands of geese fly over our home. It is not unusual to see large flocks flying overhead in their characteristic V-shaped formation. Friends have told me that these geese cover about 70 percent more distance together than if they were flying alone. They go farther and faster, and they are safer when they travel together. The same truth applies to discipleship. Growing as a disciple has a personal dimension, but it is not a private experience. We grow as disciples by learning together how to be members of the body of Christ.

Such a view is theologically consistent with a Christian understanding of baptism and the church. God saves God's people. We are saved individually as we become part of the people whom God is saving. According to Paul, the Spirit is not given to individual Christians as a matter of private ecstasy or individual virtue. God bestows the Spirit first of all upon the whole community: "There are varieties of gifts, but the same Spirit; and there are varieties of services, but the same Lord; and there are varieties of activities, but it is the same God who activates all of them in everyone. To each is given the manifestation of the Spirit for the common good" (1 Cor. 12:4-7). We possess a share of this Spirit by virtue of our participation in the body of Christ.

We understand the social dimension of Christian faith when we reflect on doctrines such as baptism or the Holy Spirit. But we revert to our default positions of individualism and consumerism when planning for discipleship development. We assume that if we help people grow individually, if we pour enough information into their heads, if we give them enough personally meaningful experiences, then they will inevitably grow as disciples of Jesus Christ. This approach assumes they will grow on their own if we just give them the resources and space. It assumes that all people need is information. Information, however, never moves people beyond the first phases of the discipleship journey. For formation and transformation to occur, something else is needed.

The squirrels that scamper across my yard have no difficulty being squirrels. They are born with instincts that tell them how to climb trees, swing from branches, and bury acorns. Human beings, on the other hand, have to construct their identities. We choose how we will live and the impact we want to have upon the world. We each must construct an identity that tells us who we are. We assemble this identity so we can answer the questions "Who am I?" and "What am I to do in this situation?"

We do not construct our identities in isolation, however. They emerge from the formative and transformative give-and-take of social relationships. We are members of various groups and communities that form and transform how we think, behave, and envision our world. Some groups or communities are small and intimate, such as our families. Others are much larger: the region of the country or part of the world where we live, the place we work, the social networks in which we participate. To a large extent, our membership in various communities of practice defines who we are.

This communal, relational process of making meaning is the basic process of learning. Learning means making, remaking, and discovering new meanings that guide our thinking and behaving. These processes occur primarily through social interactions and relationships. To say that we become disciples of Jesus Christ by apprenticing ourselves as members of a discipling community is to acknowledge that our identities as disciples of Jesus Christ develop in the same way that all human identity develops.

Individualistic and consumerist approaches to discipleship are not only theologically incorrect, but they contradict what Orr, Dreyfus and Dreyfus, and other researchers report about how people learn specific communal practices. They also ignore what we know about how human identity is formed and transformed. Followers of Jesus are more than individual consumers of knowledge and skills. Congregations have a responsibility to create safe, open, and relational spaces where disciples at all stages of the journey can share their experiences, work in relationships that emphasize care for others and for all God's creation, and be continually introduced to new, transformative ways of loving, knowing, and serving God and neighbor.

INADEQUATE APPROACHES TO BECOMING A MEMBER OF A DISCIPLING COMMUNITY

Congregations have relied on the Sunday school since the nineteenth century to create social environments where people can learn Christian practices and grow as followers of Jesus Christ. This approach increasingly faces several challenges as we enter the twenty-first century.

The Sunday School and Its Challenges

First, many congregations no longer regard the Sunday school as a sustainable model. Shifting demographics have diminished the pool of potential teachers. Adults often view the Sunday school as a setting exclusively for children and youth. Single-parent households have limited discretionary time and energy. Dual-income households also feel constrained by time and energy. Our obsession with 24-7 availability squeezes time for both leisure and sabbath out of our lives. Long commutes further diminish free time and erode our connections to neighbors and community institutions. Consequently, churches—particularly small and midsize congregations—increasingly lack sufficient teachers and a critical mass of participants.

Second, the Sunday school model relies on individualistic and consumerist assumptions about adult learning. Participants are viewed as individual consumers who shop for classes that sound interesting to them. Leaders assume people are motivated by rational self-interest and will seek the best goods and services that interest them. From their perspective, shopping for a Sunday school class is no different than shopping for a pair of shoes or a new car. Faced with a bewildering hodgepodge of classes and groups, learners are left on their own to make meaning out of whatever knowledge they acquire. They acquire information, but they do not necessarily experience this knowledge in a formative—let alone transformative—way. This approach to adult discipleship formation also undermines any sense of membership in a community of shared practice where people are mentors and apprentices to one another.

Third, the Sunday school format may inadvertently block people from growing beyond committed membership. Commitment to a particular class is equated with faithful discipleship. Our unspoken message may be: So long as you are committed to regular Sunday school attendance, you are doing everything necessary to be a follower of Jesus Christ.

In this sense, we have inadvertently created a particularly unhelpful church culture in North America. We have created a culture that regards people's spiritual lives as an individual, personal matter. Therefore, church members avoid explicitly testifying or witnessing to others and consequently seldom invite people to come and follow Jesus. Simultaneously, we have created a church culture that is low in challenge. Leaders are reluctant to challenge their own members to grow as disciples for fear they will take offense and go elsewhere—taking their money and talents with them. This low-invitation/low-challenge culture results in committed membership becoming the expected norm in most congregations.

The Limitations of Small-Group Ministries

Some church leaders consequently have abandoned the Sunday school as a vehicle for adult discipleship formation. They have instead embraced small-group ministries as their basic strategy.

Small groups provide many benefits. They can assimilate and integrate new people into a congregation. They are contexts for supportive relationships. They provide face-to-face settings where followers of Jesus can covenant together for mutual accountability. If there is anything the church does not lack, it is small groups. In some cases, the emphasis on having a certain percentage of members in small groups or a certain number of new groups each year results in many small groups becoming indistinguishable from the traditional topically-oriented short-term Sunday school class. In other cases, small groups are co-opted by the ethos of 12-step groups. They become settings for mutual support without much challenge or accountability. Because small groups are so effective in building commitment to the group and its members, this commitment can become an end in itself, thus blocking any development beyond committed membership.

Small-group ministries thus suffer from many of the same limitations that characterize the Sunday school. First, many of the resources for small-group ministries have a strong programmatic emphasis. Leaders must spend considerable time and energy on starting, organizing, and supervising small groups. Staff are hired and volunteers mobilized to implement a largely top-down program that can divert scarce resources from other congregational priorities.

Second, some approaches to small-group ministry suggest fixed sequences of small-group experiences. Newcomers must participate in basic or introductory short-term groups before they can select from a smorgasbord of elective small-group experiences. One's admission as a church member or election as a church officer is contingent upon having completed a certain number of small-group experiences. Certain groups are reserved for advanced disciples; others, for beginners. This approach is effective in teaching discipleship practices, but it may not apprentice people into a community that is growing in the love, knowledge, and service of God and neighbor.

Third, the small-group approach can be seen as little more than an updating of the traditional Sunday school model. While the Sunday school scheduled all its classes or groups synchronously at one place and time, the small-group model allows groups to meet at various locations and times throughout the week. If the Sunday school with its age-specific classes and graded curriculum modeled itself on the twentieth-century elementary school, the small-group model—with its basic and advanced classes, its introductory experiences and elective groups—resembles twentieth-century American higher education where students took basic courses as prerequisites to more advanced ones. Viewed from a certain perspective, both small-group ministry and the Sunday school rely on twentieth-century American models of formal education, even as the church enters the second decade of the twenty-first century amid different circumstances.

Fourth, small-group approaches frequently presume a large congregation with extensive resources and sufficient staff or volunteers to coordinate a complex, dynamic system. Leaders of small or mid-size congregations often read the books explaining how to implement a small-group approach and feel overwhelmed. They perceive the resource requirements to be far beyond their congregation's capacity. If the Sunday school model no longer seems sustainable, the small-group model may not be scalable. Leaders of small and midsize congregations feel unable to scale down models seemingly appropriate for larger churches. Looking at what is required, they give up before they begin.

Fifth, if the Sunday school sometimes creates a low-invitation/low-challenge culture, many small-group ministries inadvertently create a culture that is high-invitation/low-challenge. Church leaders actively encourage people to form new groups and invite others to join them. Since many small groups adopt the values of support and mutual care, the result can be a low-challenge environment. Once invited into the group, members are not challenged to grow. Accountable discipleship groups are probably the one exception to this danger. Accountable discipleship groups are intentionally high-challenge settings. In a sense, they may be the exception that proves the rule.

Neither of these models adopts a holistic approach that informs, forms, and transforms in the same way that being apprenticed into a disciplining community does. If we want different results, we need to bring a new level of intentionality to how we apprentice people into a community of shared practice. Congregations exist to be a sign, foretaste, and instrument of God's reign. They do not exist to create and maintain a certain number of classes or have a particular percentage of members in small groups. One question congregational leaders face is how to create a teaching and learning environment that is both high-invitation and high-challenge.

To What Community Will We Apprentice Ourselves?

Both the Sunday school and small-group ministries share another deficiency. They mistakenly assume that having people in groups ensures that they are learning what the church hopes they will learn. Unfortunately, many small groups and Sunday school classes live by secular norms and identities rather than kingdom practices. These settings have sometimes been co-opted by secular practices that are based on our society's hyperindividualism, materialism, and consumerism.

We are all members of some community of shared practice. From the day we were born, we have been learning how to be members of one or more communities of shared practice. According to Paul, the question facing us is a simple one: To which community do we commit ourselves? We can be members of Adam's body, the first man who fell into envy, rivalry, suspicion, and violence (Rom. 5:19); or we can apprentice ourselves to the body of Christ.

People come to the church already shaped by cultural practices grounded in a marred creation. Bringing these practices into the church, they reshape its life into the image of their everyday world, a world disfigured by desire, rivalry, and hostility. This process is no different than Israel's demand for a king. Israel ceased to be an alternative society that embodied God's style of ruling the world. It instead remade itself into just another ancient kingdom no different from those of the Canaanites and Philistines around it. In the same way, the church—rather than being salt and light for the world—uncritically adopts society's practices of competitiveness and rivalry, individualism and materialism.

In so doing, practices of hospitality and generosity, outreach and service, are abandoned. Being the church with the latest technology pushes out the practice of simplicity. Congregations compete to have the best programs, the most small groups, or the highest worship attendance. Rather than trusting God's abundance and living with hospitality and generosity, congregations hoard resources and fear scarcity. They consequently cease to be plausible, transforming signs of God's reign.

Christian community is a shared social space where we critique the practices into which our culture socializes us and learn new practices that embody our calling as disciples of Jesus Christ. Unlearning old habits is sometimes harder than learning new ones. Paul's Corinthian correspondence reflects precisely this dual process of critique and apprenticeship, of unlearning and relearning. Paul's controversies frequently revolved around a congregation's refusal to unlearn the old creation's social practices that contradicted the kingdom practices into which he had apprenticed his converts.

Paul taught his Corinthian congregation gospel practices of generosity and hospitality, particularly at the community's shared meal. Unfortunately, rich members brought their secular meal practices into the church. Rather than a practice of hospitality, generosity, and inclusion, the rich were practicing the patterns that characterized Hellenistic meals. These practices reinforced social and economic divisions between the rich and the poor. Paul wrote to critique these practices and to call church members back to their practice of hospitality and generosity.

We too sometimes import the practices of a disfigured creation into the church. The church is meant to be a sign, foretaste, and instrument of God's reign; but we change it into an image of our present world's patterns of envy, competition, and hostility. In Romans 12, Paul tells his readers, "I appeal to you therefore, brothers and sisters, by the mercies of God, to present your bodies as a living sacrifice, holy and acceptable to God, which is your spiritual worship. Do not be conformed to this world, but be transformed by the renewing of your minds, so that you may discern what is the will of God—what is good and acceptable and perfect" (vv. 1-2).

The more that leaders focus on helping people learn to become members of a community of shared gospel practices, the more they will build people's capacity to critique old practices and acquire new ones. Responding in a biblical way does not come naturally. It requires practice. Chesley Sullenberger landed his jetliner on the Hudson River and avoided a disastrous crash. He was able to carry out a nearly perfect water landing because he had practiced it again and again. We similarly practice our way to discipleship. When we are apprenticed into a discipling community, we find ourselves in relational groups that embody the gospel and make it real. Growth as a disciple of Jesus Christ comes when we create environments that generate an alternative future for the world and invite people to enter and dwell within this alternative reality so as to establish God's kingdom on earth as it is in heaven.

APPRENTICED INTO A COMMUNITY OF SHARED PRACTICE

We live in an era of hungry hearts and lonely, restless minds. Further tinkering around the edges of our strategies for making disciples of Jesus Christ for the transformation of the world cannot produce the results we seek. The shaping of the twenty-first century remains as yet unclear. We do know, however, that the crises and opportunities we face globally, environmentally, socially, and personally will require new, imaginative responses.

One response to our era's hungry hearts and restless minds has been to revitalize Sunday schools. Unfortunately, numerous demographic forces work against these efforts. Small-group strategies have sought to overcome these same difficulties by adopting a different approach. Yet these small-group strategies can further compartmentalize people's lives. Groups and classes for mutual support, education, or fellowship go about their tasks, sometimes ordering themselves by cultural rather than gospel values. Meanwhile decision-making and enabling structures of the church order their work according to secular models and unexamined cultural presuppositions. Mission groups operate in another silo, focusing on the world's needs and acts of justice or compassion. Christian education is left with the task of discipleship formation.

We are consequently given contradictory, confusing messages about what practices really characterize a disciple's life. It is time to undertake a more thorough revisioning of how we make disciples of Jesus Christ for the transformation of the world.

Four Criteria for a New Approach

Any new approach will be required to meet at least four conditions. First, it must be *sustainable*. Sustainability asks, "Are there sufficient resources and people to maintain this project for the long haul?" Too often congregations undertake initiatives, only to see them fade in a few months or years because they lack sufficient time, people, and resources to maintain them. Models are introduced that cannot be sustained beyond a single generation. Subsequent generations feel the weight of these models but are reluctant to abandon them even when they recognize their unsustainability.

Second, any new approach must be *scalable*. Congregations must be able to scale any new model to their particular context. Scalability asks, "Can this concept be adjusted for congregations of all sizes?" Can the basic idea be scaled to a large membership urban congregation as well as to a rural chapel?

Third, any new model will acknowledge that change occurs through many small steps. No quick-fix, out-of-the-box solution exists. Effective solutions are local and evolve naturally. They are "bottom-up" rather than top-down. Top-down, single-priority changes typically fail because they encounter people's natural resistance. The diversity within many congregations exacerbates this resistance and dooms most change initiatives before they even begin.

Finally, any new approach will focus on the whole congregation's responsibility for how it practices an intentional, disciplined faith. Leaders will give priority attention to forming a community of shared practice where disciples of Jesus Christ are apprentices and mentors to one another. They will focus on the whole congregational system rather than its parts. This strategy will not supersede the Sunday school or small-group ministries but instead subsume them into a more comprehensive framework.

It is not enough to help people engage in discipleship practices on their own. The critical task is to create environments that invite people to become members of a community of shared practice—the body of Christ. Church leaders can no longer think they are doing enough if they have some Sunday school classes and maybe a midweek group or two. They must instead be skilled in networking and social communication and know how to draw diverse people into relationships of faithful communal practice. They must think relationally rather than programmatically. They envision the whole life of the church as a school of discipleship—a place where ongoing growth and struggle are expected and where a normative vision of the Christian life as a life grounded in Jesus' announcement of God's inbreaking reign is taught, reflected upon, and practiced.

FOR FURTHER REFLECTION

Using the diagram on the next page (fig. 4.3), place a dot that indicates the level at which you see your performance on each line representing a discipleship practice. Then connect the dots with a solid line.

RELATIONSHIP BETWEEN MY DISCIPLESHIP PRACTICES AND DISCIPLESHIP STAGES

- What does the resulting pattern suggest to you about your discipleship practice?
- What might it suggest about your phase of discipleship?
- Are there steps you could take to grow in one or more practices? (Do not try to take big leaps, moving from a cautious seeker to a tested disciple. Ask simply what it would take to go from a curious inquirer to a committed member.)

FIGURE 4.3
Personal Inventory of My Discipleship Practices and Stages

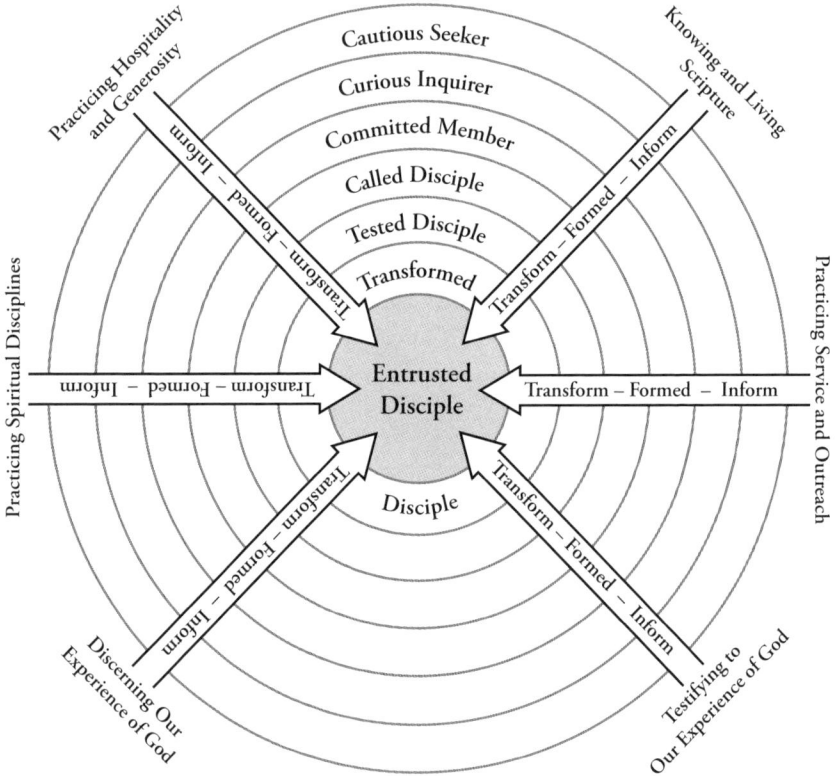

Cautious Seeker
Curious Inquirer
Committed Member
Called Disciple
Tested Disciple
Transformed
Disciple

Entrusted Disciple

Practicing Hospitality and Generosity
Knowing and Living Scripture
Practicing Spiritual Disciplines
Practicing Service and Outreach
Discerning Our Experience of God
Testifying to Our Experience of God

Transform – Formed – Inform

Using the matrix on the next page (fig. 4.4), list all the groups, classes, councils, boards, and committees in your congregation in the left column. Then in the row associated with each group, describe in each cell how that group encourages growth in the column's discipleship practice.

- What do you notice about the distribution of groups and practices? Do learning groups engage in certain practices that never occur in doing or decision-making groups? Or are some practices limited only to doing or ministry-oriented groups? What does this pattern suggest?
- Are there some practices in which no groups or only few groups engage?
- Are there some practices that are happening in almost all groups?
- Is it possible for someone to be involved in the congregation but have limited exposure to the full range of discipleship practices?
- Do people in certain phases of discipleship development tend to cluster in certain groups or types of groups? For example, where are committed disciples most likely to appear? Entrusted disciples? Curious inquirers?
- What groups are attracting curious inquirers and what practices do they learn in these settings?
- If you were to take one or two steps that would enhance your congregation's capacity to help people become members of your community of shared discipleship practices, what would you do? What would be the first step?

FIGURE 4.4

GROUP	Studying the Bible	Practicing spiritual disciplines	Practicing hospitality and generosity	Engaging in service and outreach	Reflecting on the experience of God in one's life	Testifying or witnessing to God's presence in one's life
Example: Stewardship committee	Has 10 minute Bible study at each meeting	Agrees to pray for one another and church stewardship each Tuesday at 7:30 a.m				During stewardship campaign shares with congregation how tithing has made a difference in their lives.

CHAPTER FIVE

PRACTICING TOGETHER

Knowledge has a context, and learning is situated in this context. A group of baseball players meets after school for team practice; later that evening, each player goes home and rehearses how to swing the bat, catch the ball, or slide home. They learn best how to bat, pitch, and catch at the same time and in the same context as they learn to play as a team. People often practice together before they practice alone. In a certain sense, learning to play baseball does not happen inside the individual player's head. It occurs in the relationship between the individual and the team.

As a child, I learned to play a flute. Most of my weekly individual lessons were spent reviewing and rehearsing the music I would be performing at concerts. Conversely, when I rehearsed with the entire band, I would usually discover where my own individual performance needed further work. Learning to play the flute required this rhythm of practicing together and practicing alone. I did not learn to play the flute in isolation, but rather in the relationship between the band and me.

Learning to be a disciple of Jesus Christ—like learning to play baseball or perform in a band—is both an individual undertaking and a communal endeavor. We do not learn to be Christians on our own. We learn to be disciples of Jesus Christ as part of his body, the church. Learning to be a disciple occurs in the relationship between an individual and the body of Christ. Becoming a Christian means apprenticing oneself into a community of shared practice. To understand learning, it is necessary to focus on the community where this learning takes place. Individual learning is inseparable from shared practice because knowledge is socially constructed and distributed. The central unit of analysis for teaching and learning discipleship is the intersection of personal identity and community membership.

THREE FEATURES OF COMMUNITIES OF SHARED PRACTICE

Etienne Wenger and others have pioneered a way of understanding organizations as "communities of practice" where social learning occurs (Snyder and Wenger 2010). All communities of shared practice exhibit three basic characteristics: (1) mutual engagement; (2) shared practice; and (3) common vocabulary, symbols, and tools. Congregations need these same three characteristics to be discipling communities. They need clear access to one another's lives in both formal and informal settings (mutual engagement). They need a particular process or vehicle through which they learn together (shared practice). And they need a shared language of discipleship (common vocabulary, symbols, and tools).

Mutual Engagement—Access to One Another's Lives

Mutual engagement describes the presence of multiple opportunities for informal conversation and sharing. Through mutual engagement, people have access to one another's lives. Informal settings encourage people to build personal relationships, to discover common interests, and to establish networks for sharing knowledge. Mutual engagement creates informal environments where people construct their own groups and learning networks. In these settings, mentors and apprentices naturally find one another. Orr's photocopier technicians, for example, learned to be members of a community of shared practice as they informally shared meals, gathered for coffee breaks, and spent time together en route to repairs.

Human conversation is one of the most ancient ways people have cultivated the conditions for change. When people talk to one another about what matters to them, they begin to come alive. Conversations are the creative source from which new visions of the future emerge. As people share insights among themselves in informal settings, a sense of the whole gradually becomes more accessible to everyone.

Congregational leaders usually devote most of their time and energy to formal groups that appear on an organizational chart. Self-organizing groups, on the other hand, hardly draw their attention. Yet these informal groupings represent important arenas out of which partnerships in the gospel emerge. Church leaders give scant attention to these settings because they are usually rewarded for activities that can be counted or measured, and formal groups or classes are easier to quantify. Mutual engagement also requires a different skill set. Leaders must be highly relational, skilled in social networking, and attentive to subtle signals in the environment.

One midsize congregation rethought its midweek Advent and Lenten worship services after several years of declining attendance. Seasonal midweek worship was moved from the sanctuary to the fellowship hall. Participants gathered at round tables instead of sitting in pews. Singing, Bible study, and common prayer happened around these same tables. These events provided an informal opportunity for natural groupings of apprentices and mentors to emerge.

Both the participants and those preparing the meals were given access to one another's lives. Different committees were assigned an evening when they would provide a light supper for participants. Committee members thus found themselves interacting in new ways. Rather than sitting in a conference room discussing a preset agenda, they worked side by side and shared information about themselves that they had not previously disclosed. In the same way, sharing food and conversation at round tables encouraged a different quality of interaction among church members. Out of these table conversations, people discovered common interests and forged new relationships. In some cases, these relationships became the basis for new ministry groups. Some parents with small children, for example, now meet regularly for support after having first met at these gatherings. A group of older, single women discovered they shared a common interest in cooking. They now gather regularly to share a meal and engage in Bible study.

These apprenticeships in the gospel were not top-down initiatives. They developed bottom-up within a carefully designed framework that maximized informal sharing and networking. *This approach required congregational leaders who were attuned to informal conversation, encouraged follow-up, and provided support and resources for emergent groups.*

Mutual engagement creates a rhythm of different occasions where people can gather and discover opportunities for collaboration. One congregation restructured its coffee hour to increase opportunities for conversation and relationship building among its participants. Coffee and other drinks were moved from a distant fellowship hall to an adjacent room where the congregation worshiped. Leaders removed furniture that created barriers to interaction. Themed celebrations were introduced periodically to attract curious worshipers to participate. Coffee hour now represents an informal environment where mentoring, coaching, and apprenticeship naturally unfold.

Welcoming different levels of participation plays a critical role in mutual engagement. Some people will always be core participants. Others stay actively engaged but remain outside the core membership. Still others attend only as peripheral participants. Informal settings that mix all types of participants are crucial to forming relationships that foster discipleship growth.

Peripheral participation creates opportunities for curious inquirers and committed members to find the right relationship at the right time with the right disciple who can guide them toward greater growth. Such pairings of mentors and apprentices cannot be managed or forced into a mold. They are an emergent phenomenon. Both the reformatting of coffee hour and the redesigned midweek worship reflect this intentional mixing of peripheral participants with active members and core leaders.

Formal, programmatic approaches to discipleship development tend to segregate peripheral participants from active and core members. Active and core members frequently congregate together, unintentionally excluding those on the periphery. A congregation's active core can sometimes delegitimize peripheral participants, labeling them as "Christmas and Easter" Christians. This dismissive attitude results in taking cautious seekers and curious inquirers out of consideration when planning new initiatives. Both seasoned disciples and peripheral seekers are deprived of opportunities to discover one another's gifts and to form collaborative apprenticeships in the gospel.

One congregation has eliminated the word *newcomer* from its bulletin, newsletter, and other communications. Leaders felt that describing an event as something for "newcomers" discouraged active members from attending. The vocabulary of newcomers and members created a "we vs. them" attitude, which undermined a sense of community. Leaders instead speak of "circles of participation." Their goal is to provide many settings where legitimate peripheral participation is encouraged so that newer participants have an opportunity to build relationships with active members and core leaders.

In another congregation, church officers who were rotating off the church council felt left out and abandoned. They had been at the center of communication and information for three years. Now they were on the outside looking in. Leaders responded by creating a special reception shortly after new officers were installed. This reception included both outgoing council members and peripheral participants in the congregation. Church leaders promoted the event as an opportunity to thank officers for their service. They made a special effort to invite curious seekers and committed members. The event included a meal and a guest speaker. Planners assigned everyone to mixed tables so that outgoing officers, active members, and peripheral participants had an opportunity to get to know one another better.

At one year's reception, some participants discovered that they shared a common interest in contemporary film and theological reflection. They created a small group that now meets monthly to share a meal, watch a film, and discuss its implications for their faith. This group did not emerge in a preplanned, top-down fashion. Church leaders did not initiate it because they decided it would be good for the church. They did not impose it because it was part of the latest program initiative. The group bubbled up from collaborative relationships that were part of a strategy of mutual engagement.

Still another congregation has moved away from thinking programmatically about discipleship formation. Its leaders instead believe relationship building and one-on-one mentoring are the primary ways to develop disciples of Jesus Christ. This congregation's leaders have not abandoned small groups and the Sunday school. Instead, they have sought to set these programs within a larger framework of mentoring and apprenticeship. They see these two approaches as mutually reinforcing and complementary. Small groups and Sunday school classes are no longer expected to carry the full burden of discipleship formation. Apprenticeships in the gospel stimulate the formation of new groups and classes. Participation in small groups and Sunday school classes prepares people for one-on-one mentoring and apprenticeship. Each setting benefits and reinforces the other because learning to be a Christian ultimately takes place in the network of relationships between the individual and the community. The result has been a "both/and" solution rather than a choice between small groups or Sunday school and strategies of mutual engagement.

Mutual engagement meets the five criteria for a new approach to nurturing disciples of Jesus Christ. It is sustainable because it does not require a long-term investment of resources that subsequent generations may find difficult to maintain. Because it is bottom-up, it is scalable. The extent of informal settings are determined by the size and scale of the congregation. Mutual engagement does not presume to be a quick-fix solution. Initiatives are local and emerge slowly over time. Finally, this approach does not eliminate small groups or the Sunday school; rather, it subsumes them into a larger framework that focuses on building relationships among people at different stages of their discipleship journeys. When people have access to one another's lives, apprenticeships in the gospel naturally emerge.

Shared Practice

Without shared practice, the principle of mutual engagement could become just another strategy for drawing individual disciples into new adult classes or small groups. Shared practice prevents this outcome, however. Shared practice describes how the church as a whole incorporates practicing alone and practicing together into one mutually interdependent dynamic. Shared practice is the vehicle through which people learn together.

We usually envision learning as the cognitive residue of meaning left inside someone's head after certain experiences. This viewpoint turns the individual learner into the locus of learning. But it is practicing together that informs, forms, and transforms someone's individual performance. From this perspective, learning no longer "belongs" to the individual learner. The locus of learning shifts to the relationship between the individual and the community of shared practice. Learning takes place in the space between the individual learner and the community. When we say that learning occurs in the space between the individual and the community, we are saying that learning is fundamentally a contextual and relational mode of knowing, not a personal transaction inside our heads.

Knowledge, attitudes, skills, and habits do not ultimately belong to the individual learner or practitioner. I can learn to play baseball, but that does not make me a baseball player on a team. Being a team baseball player or member of the orchestra means being part of a community that together engages in a whole ensemble of practices where the whole is greater than the sum of its parts. Learning happens at the intersection of the personal and the social. It is not a deposit of information in our heads. Learning both arises from and resides within relationships of mutual discovery and shared experience.

Discipleship does not occur as a deposit of ideas and information in my head or as a behavioral stimulus-and-response event in my body. Discipleship is what a community does as its shared practice. Shared practice involves formation and transformation as well as information. This is precisely why God calls a community into existence in order to transform the world. Faithful people covenant together to practice a way of life—a whole repertoire of knowledge, attitudes, skills, and behaviors that embody God's new creation. This whole community is the domain for a shared practice. We learn to participate in God's mission as we learn to be members of this community, learning to do what this community does.

Discipleship is what the whole people of God do together. The primary task of church leaders is to help the whole congregation grow as a discipling community in ways that simultaneously foster individual growth. Developing and forming disciples of Jesus Christ for the transformation of the world involves all parts of the congregational system. All formal and informal congregational settings engage each and every member as both teacher and learner, mentor and apprentice, across the whole life span in sharing faith together.

Church leaders must wear bifocals. They must see close up and far away, see individual members and the body as a whole. They must keep their eyes on the relational spaces where the personal and the social intersect. Their task is similar to my band director's task of helping me simultaneously learn to play the flute and perform as a member of the band. This task demands a shift of mind. Leaders who make this shift will understand discipleship formation as something that happens in the relationship between individual disciples and the congregation rather than something that occurs solely inside the individual.

We are informed, formed, and transformed as disciples as we participate in the whole life of the congregation. If the whole life of the congregation is not informed, formed, and transformed as a domain of shared practice, individual participants within it will not experience the full possibilities of growth in Christ. Church leaders help disciples grow when they enable the whole congregation to become a domain for shared practice and carefully attend to how individual disciples interact and grow within it.

In one congregation, leader orientation sessions and new teacher trainings include a module on discipleship stages and practices. Each leader or teacher is asked to think about how her or his group incorporates this model into its life and work:

- How do the six discipleship practices show up in my meetings, classes, or groups?
- What stages of discipleship are represented in my groups?
- What am I doing to develop disciples of Jesus Christ?
- How can I introduce practices that foster growing disciples in everything I do as a church leader?

Leaders and teachers brainstorm ways that, over the course of a year's meetings and classes, participants in every setting can engage in all six discipleship practices to one degree or another. Each gathering need not follow a rigid repetition of every practice. Such an approach, in fact, would be counterproductive. But, over the course of a year, members of all groups engage in a range of practices that the congregation has identified as essential for making disciples. One committee chair now asks members to read a devotional book together during Lent. In one adult Sunday school class, members have agreed to fast from the same meal each week and to contribute what they would have spent for food toward a mission project. A third chairperson uses *lectio divina* at the beginning of all meetings and invites members to use the same practice of devotional reading between meetings.

A hologram is an image in which each smaller part of the larger image contains an image of the whole. When you cut a photograph in half, each half contains a portion of the original picture. When you cut a hologram in half, the whole picture can still be seen in each part. This is because the light captured in a hologram is light scattered from every point in the scene. In a photograph, the light captured has come from only one point in the scene. In the same way, if the church is a community of shared practice, then each part contains the whole domain's practice. Everything leaders do in their groups, classes, committees, and councils shapes both the individual participant's discipleship and the whole congregation's shared practice. Both are critical because learning occurs not in one place or the other, but in the relationship between the two.

Each circle in our stage model of discipleship represents a stage on the way to entrusted discipleship. Everyone in the congregation is orbiting in one of these circles. Some participants are in the circle of cautious inquiry, others are in committed membership, and still others are in the circle of transformed disciples. As people orbit in these circuits, they pass through various groups and committees where they encounter discipleship practices meant to inform, form, and transform them as disciples of Jesus Christ. Each point of intersection between a practice and a circuit is like the turn in the labyrinth's path. It becomes an opportunity for a practice to propel someone into another circuit closer to entrusted discipleship. Each encounter with a particular discipleship practice is a moment of truth that contains within itself the potential to catapult someone into another phase of discipleship (see fig. 5.1).

FIGURE 5.1
"Moments of Truth" in Shared Practices

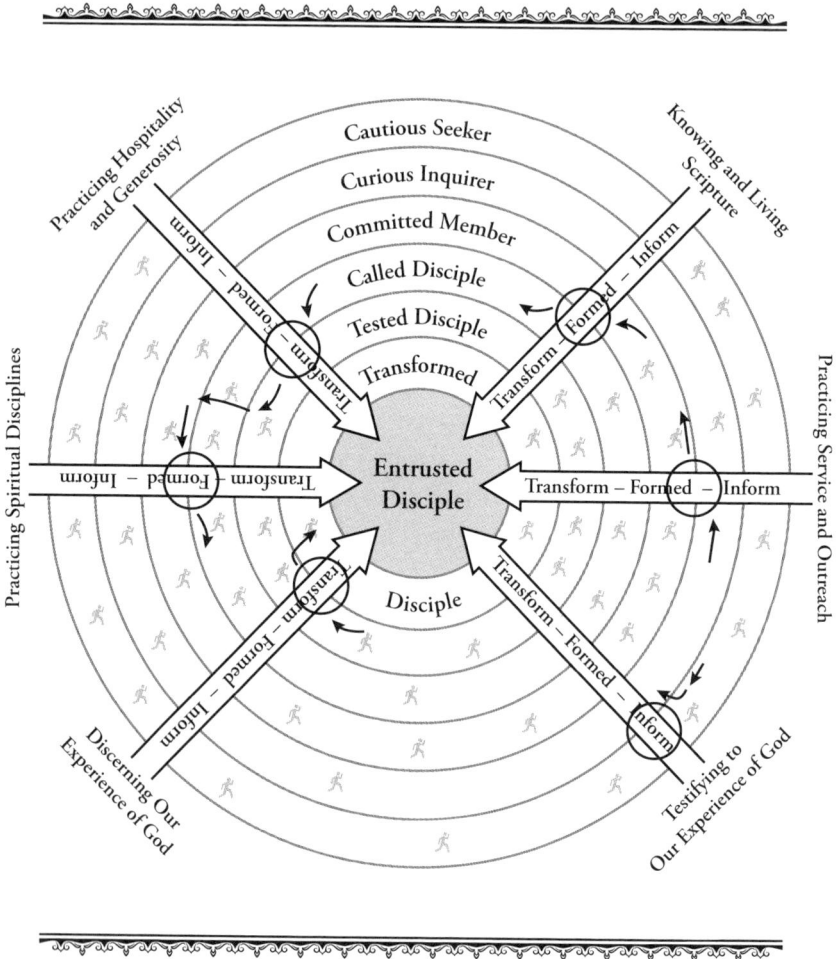

"MOMENTS OF TRUTH" IN SHARED PRACTICE

We never know which setting or practice will exercise the gravitational pull that draws someone into a circuit closer to entrusted discipleship. Therefore, every group and setting needs to maximize opportunities for people to experience the full range of discipleship practices that can inform, form, and transform them as disciples of Jesus Christ.

Congregational leaders have a special responsibility for interpreting the congregation's life as a single, unified discipleship domain. Like a hologram, the whole congregation and each of its parts incarnate what it means to receive and dwell within God's kingdom. Each setting is a microcosm of the whole congregation's discipleship practices. Each gathering becomes a place where I learn what it means to be a member of a community of shared practice. My learning occurs in the relationship between my own personal discipleship practices and the congregation's shared practices.

Like mutual engagement, shared practice is sustainable and scalable. Congregations of every size can discover ways to share together in one mission, regardless of their specific task or particular location. Shared practice is also a long-term process and works from the bottom up. It does not abrogate small-group ministries or the Sunday school, but instead establishes a new relationship between these settings and other aspects of congregational life. For these reasons, shared practice meets the criteria for a new approach to developing disciples of Jesus Christ for the transformation of the world.

Common Symbols, Vocabulary, and Tools

Disciples can rehearse together only when they share a common vocabulary that allows them to coordinate their shared practice. People need common tools and symbols to engage one another in relationships of trust and care. The absence of shared vocabulary, tools, and symbols will therefore undermine both shared practice and mutual engagement.

Most congregations do not share a common set of symbols and tools. Various groups within the congregation use different vocabulary, tools, and symbols because they are exposed to different environments and people. The mission committee frames its work in terms of "serving the least of our brothers and sisters." The evangelism committee invokes the language of "lost sheep" and "saving souls." The finance committee draws on parables and sayings that describe "the steward." The Christian education committee speaks of "making disciples." If we were to analyze the conflicts and misunderstandings that occur in churches, we would see that they often arise from competition or miscommunication caused by contradictory symbols, tools, and vocabularies lodged in different parts of the congregation.

The situation is still more complicated, however. Groups in different parts of the congregation do not merely hold conflicting biblical vocabularies and symbols. They also use different tools and vocabularies that they have imported from the culture at large. An education committee speaks of graded curriculum and cognitive development. A small-group ministry uses the vocabulary and tools of support groups or 12-step programs. The mission committee discusses an issue in terms of social analysis. Finance committees and governing boards use business terminology. Diverse vocabularies make it easy for one group to misunderstand or misinterpret what another is saying.

Furthermore, symbols and tools imported from the surrounding culture are usually not critiqued in light of the congregation's understanding of its domain of shared Christian practice. People introduce secular tools and vocabularies because they represent "how we do things" in our everyday lives. Unfortunately, the way we do things in a fallen, disfigured creation is not how God intends for the world to be. Rather than present a visible, plausible sign of God's reign, the church simply reflects the world around it with all its rivalries, desires, suspicions, and hostilities.

Healthy communities of Christian faith build a common language and tool kit for discipleship. They critique their vocabulary, symbols, and tools in light of the gospel's commandment to make disciples of Jesus Christ for the transformation of the world. Without such a critique, congregations import practices that contradict the gospel just as Paul's Corinthian congregation did when it brought Hellenistic meal practices into its table fellowship. When congregations are intentional about their vocabulary, symbols, and tools, then participants share a common picture of what a disciple looks like, what growth is expected, and where to locate resources for the journey.

In one congregation, the orientation session for new participants presents a model of discipleship stages and practices. This model is shared and practiced in all committees, classes, and groups throughout the year. Leaders use it as a basis for thinking about strategic planning and goal setting. Individuals within the congregation use it to assess what they need to grow as disciples. Over time, participants have developed a common set of symbols, vocabulary, and tools based on this model of discipleship development.

Group norms represent another leverage point for common symbols, tools, and language. Norms are the agreements that group members hold about what is good or bad, appropriate or inappropriate in a group. All groups have shared norms that emerge either intentionally or unintentionally. A group's norms determine the practices that members will adopt as part of the group. Norms are perhaps the most important mechanism for learning what it means to be a member of a group. If we want to observe the practices into which church participants are apprenticed, the best place to look will be the norms operative in various groups.

Church leaders give surprisingly little attention to group norms. Yet they are a high-leverage way to develop shared vocabulary, tools, and symbols. Leaders usually ask people to affirm beliefs and doctrines, but they seldom ask people to commit to a particular set of norms and practices that determine the shape of what one believes.

One congregation's leaders decided to help all groups and classes share some common vocabulary and symbols. The church council decided that it wanted all groups to develop some explicit, shared norms. In addition to the usual behavioral norms, groups included specific discipleship practices. These norms were then posted at each meeting.

No two groups had exactly the same norms. Yet all included common vocabulary, and the norms themselves were a shared tool. Every group incorporated some component of all six discipleship practices into their gatherings. Everyone slowly learned what it meant to be a member of a community of shared practice regardless of their location in the congregation or their stage of discipleship. While this intervention was clearly more "top-down" than "bottom-up," the congregation's governing board found that working on explicit behavioral covenants or group norms was a high-leverage intervention for building shared tools and symbols.

Creating common vocabulary, symbols, and tools meets the criteria for a new approach to adult discipleship formation. This approach promotes thinking that is relational and holistic rather than programmatic. It is scalable and sustainable. It cannot be prepackaged but occurs as an emergent phenomenon with appropriate encouragement and cultivation. It creates a social space where participants are apprenticed into membership in a community of shared practice—a community that God calls to be the body of Christ in and for the world.

Getting There from Here

A congregational system that makes disciples of Jesus Christ for the transformation of the world is characterized by settings where people have clear access to one another's lives in both formal and informal settings, a particular process for practicing and learning together, and a shared language of discipleship. It is like a hologram where each part contains the whole congregation's full range of discipleship practices.

Some Traps to Avoid

Church leaders face several potential pitfalls as they adopt an apprenticeship or shared-practice approach to developing disciples. First, the goal is generating movement, not activity. It is easy to confuse ends and means. The ultimate objective is a discipling community, not programs. Mutual encouragement, shared practice, and common vocabulary, symbols, and tools are not ends in themselves. They are a means to the end of forming disciples for the transformation of the world.

Second, there are no quick-fix solutions. We practice our way into discipleship by small steps, not by big prepackaged programs. No other congregation has a solution that you can copy. Each congregation must slowly, by trial and error, find what works in its particular context.

Third, church leaders can fall into the trap of believing it is the individual's responsibility to grow as a disciple. Effective discipleship formation is a responsibility of the whole body of Christ. Congregations must articulate a clear picture of what a disciple looks like, a concise definition of discipleship's stages and practices, and a map of the resources needed for the journey.

Fourth, leaders can fall into the trap of seeing scarcity rather than abundance. When leaders see only scarcity, they believe they cannot make changes because the congregation (a) does not have enough money; (b) lacks the people to implement something new; or (c) has no time to take on another project right now. Faithful leaders, on the other hand, begin with a vision of God's abundance, not human scarcity. God calls us to work with what we have, not with what we wish we had. God gifts us with everything we need to be a church that participates in God's mission to heal a marred creation—right here, right now.

Understanding the Diffusion of Change

Effective leaders also understand how new ideas spread within a social system. Three factors are important in the diffusion of new ideas: (1) the qualities of the change itself; (2) the characteristics of networks that diffuse this change; and (3) the needs of people who either embrace or resist it (Rogers 1983).

Qualities That Enable a Change to Spread. We usually think that an innovation spreads because more and more people adopt it. Actually, an innovation spreads because it is flexible enough to adapt to the ever-widening circles of people who encounter it. In other words, people do not change; the innovation changes as it spreads. This is precisely why big, prepackaged change initiatives usually do not work. Leaders typically seek to "sell" mix-and-pour solutions they want people to embrace "as is." But this approach places the focus on changing people, not on adapting the innovative idea or practice.

Changes that are adaptable share some common features:

1. They are simple to use;
2. they are compatible with people's core values;
3. they are something people can try without significant risk; and
4. people can observe the results of these changes.

An apprenticeship or shared-practice model meets these four criteria. Discipleship practices are simple to understand. They are not complicated in and of themselves. Second, these practices are consistent with the espoused values of Christian faith. Third, embedding them holographically throughout the congregation can be done without significant risk. In fact, adopting these practices may actually mitigate some risks congregations typically face. Finally, the fruit of disciplined practice can be observed in both the quality of congregational life and the character of individual disciples.

Communication Patterns and the Diffusion of Innovation. New ideas spread through peer-to-peer conversations and social networks. Peer networks are part of the phenomenon we currently call "viral marketing." This fact underlines the importance of mutual engagement. Strategies for mutual engagement both take advantage of existing peer-to-peer networks and create new networks, which can spread innovations more widely throughout an organization. The more a change effort exposes the opinion of leaders within social networks to new ideas, the higher the likelihood that people will adopt these innovations.

Population Segments That Embrace or Resist Change. Any model for diffusion of change must take into account how different groups of people respond to a possible change in their beliefs, practices, or behaviors. Change efforts encounter five distinct groups of people (Rogers 1983):

Innovators love to try something new. They enjoy being the first people who have a new technological gadget or embrace a new fad. This group accounts for about 2.5 percent of the population. If you propose something new, they will be the first ones to try it.

Early adopters like to try new things. They watch innovators carefully to know what trends are up-and-coming. Early adopters are usually the ones who work out an innovation's problems so it can appeal to a larger audience. About 13.5 percent of the population are early adopters.

New innovations next encounter a much larger group of people. This third group constitutes the *early majority*. They are typically risk-adverse and pragmatic. They do not act until they have solid proof that a new idea works with a minimum of disruption. They also want something that is "user-friendly." Once early adopters have modified an innovation so it is easy to use, the early majority will embrace it. The early majority represents about 34 percent of the organization.

The fourth group represents people who are not really comfortable with a new idea. They are the *late majority*. They reluctantly adopt any new approach, and they do so only because they want to conform to everyone else's expectations. This group also represents about 34 percent of the population.

Finally, every organization includes *laggards*. Laggards constitute about 16 percent of the population. They may never adopt an idea. They will think of every reason possible not to adopt something new; and they will be happy to tell you why it will never work.

These five population segments explain why many congregational change efforts fail. First, congregations and their leaders are frequently loath to upset people. If laggards represent one in six church members, then most change efforts die before they ever begin. A small minority of laggards can hold the whole system hostage.

Second, congregational leaders usually give their fullest attention to changing the people rather than adapting the innovation. Leaders typically see the challenge of change as a political process where they must win people's approval for a new idea. Leaders encounter more success when they instead seek to modify their new idea or innovation as it encounters various population segments, particularly the early majority. Encouraging each population segment to modify a new idea or tool is a slow, intentional process. Yet it produces better long-term results than either attempting to impose top-down changes or engaging in overt political processes that produce a short-term "win."

Third, leaders overlook the importance of worship for the diffusion of change in church systems. Church leaders often borrow concepts from the organizational behavior literature and map these methods onto congregational life. This approach undervalues the importance of worship as the central act of Christian congregations. Worship is an end in itself, and leaders ought never to consider it a means to any other end.

On the other hand, worship constitutes the primary setting where people are informed, formed, and transformed. In worship, people rehearse how to become members of a community of shared practice. In worship, people are shaped by a common set of symbols and vocabulary. From Monday through Saturday, they have engaged in discipleship alone or with others in smaller formal and informal gatherings. On Sunday, they gather to practice together.

The purpose of worship is not to send people out simply so they can return the next Sunday. Its purpose is to inform, form, and transform them so they participate in God's mission of healing a broken world. A key question for church leaders is how worship informs, forms, and transforms participants, who are together engaged in a rhythm of personal and communal discipleship practices.

Some Suggested Next Steps

The most critical transformation that discipleship development requires is a fundamental shift in the consciousness of each Christian. Disciples of Jesus Christ have to see themselves both as learners and as teachers, as apprentices and as mentors in the Christian way. Programs, groups, and classes do not develop disciples. Disciples are developed relationally. This relational process is the responsibility of every disciple.

One strategy for moving toward an apprenticeship or shared-practice approach to discipleship development includes the following three steps, which are based on Roger's (1983) theory of how innovation spreads throughout an organization or population:

1. **Build Common Vocabulary, Symbols, and Tools.** Explore with your governing board or church council how it understands (a) God's mission to the world; (b) what defines a disciple of Jesus Christ; and (c) what discipleship practices sustain the ongoing transformation of disciples who are called to transform the world. The exercises in chapters 1 and 2 can be adapted for these conversations.

Once your governing board or church council has a clear, concise, and written statement about God's mission to the world, a description of a disciple of Jesus Christ, and the practices that support and sustain discipleship, invite your council or board to develop a model for the stages and phases of discipleship. The model in chapter 3 can be a starting point. It should not be the final word, however. Encourage your governing board or church council to develop a model that reflects its own experience and context, which may be different from the one that informs this resource. Remember, every new idea has to be adapted as it encounters wider segments of the population. It cannot simply be adopted "as is." Once this second conversation is completed, your board or council will have the core components of a common vocabulary, a tool kit, and a symbol system.

Your next task is to embed this vocabulary, symbol system, and tool kit as widely as possible in your congregation. A natural place to begin is worship. Leaders can look at the language of worship as it is reflected in prayers, liturgies, and songs. How does your current language reflect your understanding of God's mission? Of discipleship? Are there ways to adjust or supplement some of your musical resources, liturgical language, and symbols to express the common vocabulary and symbols you wish to diffuse throughout the congregation? Do the words of worship and music call people to a journey of growing discipleship or encourage them to remain at the level of committed membership?

One congregation commissioned a local songwriter to produce a hymn that captured the congregation's vision and mission. This hymn was introduced into worship and sung at strategically key moments throughout the liturgical year. It was also used at congregational dinners and the annual meeting. Gradually, the symbols and vocabulary of this hymn became widely diffused at every level of the congregation.

Your governing board can also work with various formal groups to infuse new language and resources into meetings, classes, and groups. One congregation encouraged all groups and committees to begin every gathering with a time of sharing. Leaders invited people to respond to the question: Where do you see God at work in your ministry since we last met? Another congregation asked leaders to begin all gatherings by asking three questions that helped them focus on discerning God's presence in their experience and providing testimony to the hope within them:

- What has been a high moment in your life this week?
- What has been a low moment this week?
- Where have you experienced God in the midst of this week?

A third congregation invited all short-term small groups and Sunday school classes to include a brief presentation on discipleship stages at their final, wrap-up sessions. Participants were then invited to identify where they would put themselves on this map and to assess what discipleship practice or practices would be most helpful to their continuing growth as followers of Jesus Christ. With this information, leaders challenged participants to discern prayerfully what group or class they might attend next. The overarching purpose of this exercise was to move participants away from selecting short-term groups or classes solely on the basis of personal interest but rather on the basis of what would help them grow as disciples.

A fourth congregation's governing board sought to identify high-leverage settings where people were most open to new vocabulary, resources, and meanings. They identified new officer training sessions, newcomer orientations, membership classes, and organizational sessions for new Sunday school classes or small groups as important norming moments. They worked with group leaders, Sunday school teachers, and paid staff to include a module in these settings that explained the congregation's model for discipleship stages and practices and then invited participants to reflect on where they felt they were in this journey. The module concluded with an exercise in which participants developed a personal discipleship plan for their ongoing growth.

2. Build and Broaden the Conversation. By infusing shared vocabulary, symbols, and resources throughout the congregation, church leaders and governing bodies can build a foundation for discipleship as a shared practice. Each congregation can find its own way to this next step based on its size, history, leadership, and context.

The church's board or council can plot out all the formal and informal groups within the congregation. They can then place these settings on a grid that also includes the stages of discipleship. Participants next designate which groups are designed primarily for a particular stage or stages of discipleship. Such a grid is much like the one presented in chapter 3. Participants in this exercise then discuss such questions as:

- What stage of discipleship do most of our groups seem to target?
- Are there stages of discipleship that are unserved or underserved?
- Do most groups serve a particular stage? If so, what does this say to us?
- If someone is a cautious seeker or a curious inquirer, are there settings where they are introduced to the congregation?
- How does our current mix of groups and classes encourage people to grow from one stage to the next? If this is not happening, what can we do differently?
- If we are serious about making disciples of Jesus Christ, what should we be doing more of? Less of?

Input from this exercise then guides church leaders as they develop new ministries and long-range plans.

In one congregation, leaders worked with the governing board or church council to create a list of the congregation's formal groups. Rather than ask what stage of discipleship each group served, they asked what discipleship practices were happening across these settings. Their chart looked much like the one in chapter 4.

Once the chart was completed, participants asked a list of questions that included:

- What discipleship practices are being observed in most groups?
- What discipleship practices receive little attention in our groups?
- Are there ways in which certain practices are clustered among some groups of people but not others? What does this pattern suggest?
- Is there a relationship between a group's tasks or topics and the predominant stage of discipleship shared by its participants? What does this pattern (or absence of a pattern) suggest?

Leaders used the results of this conversation to develop a plan for building and broadening discipleship practices throughout the congregation. Their goal was to create a climate where each person saw himself or herself as a growing disciple, engaged relationally with others as apprentices and mentors for the sake of God's mission to transform the world.

3. Create Informal Settings for Mutual Engagement. Having examined discipleship practices in formal settings, church councils and governing boards can begin the implementation of strategies that foster mutual engagement. They will seek to create informal settings where legitimate peripheral participation naturally occurs. These settings are crucial because diffusion of change—particularly from the early adopters to the early majority—relies heavily on peer-to-peer networking and the informal conversations that emerge in these settings. Church leaders ask how these peer-to-peer networks can be mobilized to support the diffusion of innovation:

- Who are target audiences of innovators, early adopters, the early and late majorities? Who are laggards?
- In three to five years, what would we envision each of these groups doing that they are not doing now? What do we envision them no longer doing that they now do?
- How clear is each target audience about our congregation's mission? Its definition of a disciple? Its model of discipleship practices and stages? What needs to happen so that we ensure a widespread diffusion of these understandings and practices?

How church leaders answer these questions will inform their next steps in creating settings for mutual engagement. In some cases, a governing board may find it easier to begin with informal networks rather than formal groups. As they expand contact through peer-to-peer networks and informal conversations, they create the "buzz" that helps to spread a new idea or innovation. There is no one single solution to how an apprenticeship or shared-practice model develops. Everything depends upon the creativity, imagination, and energy of church leaders who seek to make disciples of Jesus Christ for the transformation of the world.

Conclusion

This approach does not require a big budget, additional staff and volunteers, or the formation of new groups or committees. It is scalable and sustainable in congregations of all sizes. What it does require is patience, courage, and tenacity. Leaders adopting this approach focus on a long-term, positive vision for the congregation as a covenant community that informs, forms, and transforms disciples of Jesus Christ for the transformation of the world.

Church leaders start by being intentional. They practice slowly and reflectively, and they work with others. As they progress, they discover new ideas for making disciples among diverse people and groups both within and outside the congregation, and they learn to adapt their initial concept as it encounters different population segments. Most of all, they know that God has already given their congregation everything it needs for making disciples of Jesus Christ who will together be a sign, foretaste, and instrument of God's reign over all creation.

FOR FURTHER REFLECTION

Review the plan for introducing an apprenticeship approach to making disciples for Jesus Christ described in this chapter. Then discuss the following questions:

- What are some steps you could take with others in your congregation to introduce a common vocabulary, symbols, and resources for making disciples and participating in God's mission? Who else needs to be involved in this process? What will be your first step?
- What are some steps you could take to diffuse a shared domain of discipleship practices throughout your congregation? Who else needs to be involved in this process? What will be your first step?
- What are some steps you could take to foster settings for mutual engagement? Who else needs to be involved in this process? What will be your first step?

References

Dreyfus, Hubert L., and Stuart E. Dreyfus. 1986. *Mind Over Machine: The Power of Human Intuition and Expertise in the Era of the Computer.* New York: Free Press.

Hargrove, Robert. 1995. *Masterful Coaching: Extraordinary Results by Impacting People and the Way They Think and Work Together.* San Francisco: Jossey-Bass/Pfeiffer.

Orr, Julian E. 1996. *Talking about Machines: An Ethnography of a Modern Job.* Ithaca, NY: Cornell University Press.

Rogers, Everett M. 1983. *Diffusion of Innovations.* 3rd ed. New York: Free Press.

Snyder, William M., and Etienne Wenger. 2010. "Our World as a Learning System: A Communities-of-Practice Approach." In *Social Learning Systems and Communities of Practice*, edited by Chris Blackmore, 107–24. London: Springer.